PRAISE FOR

It's a brave thing to write one's personal history. Shelby included so many details of his most interesting life—many of his successes and a few regrets along the way. His tone throughout is one of gratitude for his many blessings. He speaks of the opportunities he was given in life with genuine appreciation. While Shelby calls it a "Stroke of Luck" I would say it's a cultivated point of view— to focus on the positive.

I felt so taken in by so many of the Detroit accounts. My mom and dad were both around in the 1940 race riot—a truly sad chapter of our city. The Cass Tech memories were fun to read—all of us alumni felt it was the only high school around. Reading the name of Mischa Kottler brought me right back to taking lessons upstairs at his Parkside house. Even my favorite Farmington library was included:)

Mary Kay Pryce
Northville Public Schools, Northville, MI
Vocal Music 1977-2018

It was a stroke of luck that I was offered the chance to read the manuscript of Shelby Newhouse's memoir. As a multi-talented radio and TV personality and award-winning filmmaker, Shelby lived such an interesting life, making the read a real "page turner." It was difficult to put the book down. Well done!

David Jackson
President, SC Global Media Group, film and television production and distribution worldwide.

Writing a memoir is one hell of a challenge. Shelby is a very good writer. The book is full of facts presented in a very straightforward way and I found myself taking notes and rereading many passages. I think English departments might want to use it to teach writing techniques. Certainly, programs dealing with any aspect of the film industry or teaching Michigan history would want to include Shelby's book in its must-read category or on its approved reading list.

Michael Harrington
Former school administrator, Penn State instructor, Certified Mediator, and licensed professional counselor.

A remarkable story of a man overcoming all odds. I loved the inclusion of photographs, articles, and letters, and the way they were integrated with the text. They added another dimension to the already well-told and interesting narrative.

Katie Mesbergen
Bachelor's of Science in Psychology
Arizona State University

A compelling but lighthearted autobiography by one of Detroit's most prominent media figures. From early life in the South Bronx, to the beginnings of radio broadcasting, through the heyday of network television, and into the digital age, Newhouse weaves his story. His conversational narrative style frames a life story that speaks of challenge, redemption, happiness, and joy.

His career path started with pioneering on-air work in radio and TV during the '40s and '50s. It blossomed with his creation of thoughtful and imaginative commercial projects and documentary works in the late 20th century. In a delightfully self-effacing manner, he shares immersive stories and anecdotes from the "Mad Men" era of advertising. He holds back nothing, describing his relationships with industry and government leaders, colleagues in the advertising and film industry, and a host of other colorful figures.

This work will certainly appeal to readers interested in the Golden Age of media and advertising, especially as it relates to Detroit.

E. Joseph Miller
Business Agent, The Detroit Stage Employees Union,
IATSE Local 38, Vice President, Metro Detroit AFL-CIO

A STROKE OF LUCK

A STROKE OF LUCK

A Memoir
by
Shelby Z. Newhouse

PARK HAUS PRESS, LLC

This work expresses opinions and depicts actual events in the life of the author as truthfully as recollection permits and/or can be verified by research. As necessary, dialogue from conversations with the author has been scripted to express the essence of the characters involved and/or the situation. All persons within are actual individuals; there are no composite characters. The names of some individuals may have been changed to respect their privacy.

Copyright © 2023 by Christa Kindt Newhouse

All rights reserved. No part of this book may be reproduced or used by any means, graphic, electronic, cyber, or mechanical, including photocopying, recording, taping, posting, or streaming without written permission of the copyright owner, except for the use of brief quotations in critical reviews or articles.

To request permissions, contact the publisher at parkhauspress@gmail.com

Library of Congress Control Number: 2023922733

ISBN: 979-8-218-33021-7
     1. Newhouse, Shelby Z.   2. Memoir

First paperback edition December 2023.

Cover design by Steve Kruk.
Layout and editing by Paula McKinney Tucker and Christa Kindt Newhouse.
Editing, Consulting, and Legal Assistance by Dana Newhouse.

Printed in the United States of America
PublishingXpress
Madison Heights, MI 48071

Sault Ste. Marie, MI 49783

Dear Readers,

I believe the story of my life can be reduced to one phrase, "A Stroke of Luck." See if you agree.

Come with me on my journey of memories: my adventures and misadventures; behind-the-scenes and in-front-of-the-camera show-biz facts, gossip, people, and happenings; and thought-provoking stories and illuminating back-stories, recalled in their historical context, asking to be to be read, remembered, and even further researched! Perhaps by you?

Bon Voyage! I hope you enjoy!

Your host,

Shelby Z. Newhouse

IN THESE PAGES

HOW IT ALL STARTED	1
I JOIN THE CAST	5
THE TEEN YEARS	13
DISCRIMINATION ON ALL FRONTS	19
FIVE MONTHS LATER . . .	23
BACK ON THE AIR	29
A CAREER BEGINS	35
PUTTING DOWN ROOTS *Thank You Detroit News*	39
A PAUSE FOR THE PERSONAL	43
WHAT ELSE BUT AUTOMOTIVE?	51
MEADOW BROOK HALL	63
INEQUALITY AND EQUAL JUSTICE	69
BEHIND THE CAMERA	79
ORGANIZED CRIME	87
IT'S ONLY POLITICS	95
A LIGHTNING ROD FOR CONTROVERSY	101
EXPANDING HORIZONS	109
CHANGES ALL AROUND	117
MIRACLE OF THE DANCING SUN	127
SECRETS AND THE CURSE	135
OMNE TRIUM PERFECTUM . . . *Good Things Come in Threes*	143
JIMMY, HERBERT, AND THE ISLAND	149

GUESTS AND STORIES
    A Wonderful Combination   **155**

FRIENDS!   **163**

CHANGE, THE ONLY CONSTANT   **169**

VISTAS, COLOR, AND FIBER   **175**

JUST DAY TO DAY . . .   **183**

ON THE ROAD AGAIN!   **189**

ALMOST FULL CIRCLE
    (My past has made my present possible)   **197**

SHELBY ALWAYS KNEW HOW TO SAY
    "Thank You"   **201**

Source Notes   **203**

HOW IT ALL STARTED

Between the assassination of Russia's Alexander II in 1881 and the outbreak of World War II, one-third of East European Jews left Russia, Poland, Rumania, and Austro-Hungary. This migration was at once desperate and purposeful. A migration by people determined to escape conditions of hunger and persecution. Whenever problems arose, man-made or natural, drought, earthquakes, torrential rains, authorities had the answer and solution. It was always the fault of Jews. The result was genocide, massacres, and slaughter. Pogrom, after pogrom, after pogrom.

Millions tore themselves from the land. From villages where the Bible was the daily newspaper and Heaven was real. They endured the brutal conditions of the passage across the Atlantic as well as the harsh and terrifying trauma of Ellis Island's series of medical examinations: scrutinizing eyes for signs of trachoma, hair for lice, neck, arms and hands for sores or tumors. Very much aware of the possibility of being returned to the world left behind.

Today we wonder how in 1933 the scientifically and culturally advanced nation of Germany could condone Hitler's extermination of six million Jews through asphyxiation, murder, and medical experiments. Author Bella Fromm in her book "Blood and Banquets" asks, "How was it possible for the culture-loving nation of Goethe, Schiller, and Kant, of Mozart, Beethoven, Bach, and Brahms, to succumb at last to the new barbarism of Adolph Hitler?" I believe the answer is clear. This was the natural culmination of all that had gone before.

My paternal grandfather Adolph lived in a small village in Hungary. Franz Josef, Emperor of Austria-Hungary, decreed all males of a suitable age be conscripted and serve in the Royal Army. That presented a problem. The villagers of Munkács were devout Jews. But army cooks neither knew nor cared about Jewish dietary laws. Conscripts had a choice: starve or break the religious law. For the village Rabbi the solution was clear; record each male child's birth as a female. By the time the authorities learned my grandfather was a boy he was married and had five children. Of course, he was conscripted. But Grandfather had a great sense of humor. If he was meant to be a girl, so be it. It was out of his hands. He dressed as a woman, went AWOL, and traveled to London. It seems we've always been in show business!

The next stop was the McKeesport, Pennsylvania home of his brother, Joseph. But before arriving, his name was changed in typical American fashion. At Ellis Island, the immigration entry, they asked his name. He answered in Hungarian "Adolph Uiehazy." "Adolph . . . that can stay," they said, "but the Uiehazy will have to go. No one can pronounce that in this country." They asked the interpreter, "Does Uiehazy mean anything?" The answer. "A new house." "Ahhh. That's your name . . . NEWHOUSE"!

My Grandfather worked in his brother's tailor shop for eight months, earning enough money to send for his wife Rose and their five children. It was 1909. In a few years Adolph owned the town bar and one of his sons owned the pool hall. They had a lock on sin. My grandparent's youngest, born in Hungary, was 4 years old. His name was Louis. This boy grew up to be a tough kid, a wise guy of the streets of Breckinridge, Pennsylvania. It was a steel mill and blast furnace center where the fires kept the main street lit all night long. Neither his parents nor the town could hold him. Louis, "Lou" to everyone who knew him, ran away at the age of 14. I loved him and would call him Dad.

From Uiehazy to Newhouse. A plucky Grandfather, a journey of 7,600 km (4,700 mi), and my first stroke of luck.

The story of Mother's parentage reads like a novel. Her mother, Anna, was born in the city of Bialystok, a center of industry and a predominantly Jewish town in Poland. As the result of a pogrom, the killing of Jews, Anna was orphaned when she was 18. She traveled to Warsaw and went to work as a maid in the home of a wealthy Jewish tailor. *Joseph Seid!* Anna fell in love with one of his sons. What a disaster. An orphan has no dowry and no one in his right mind marries the maid! The young couple was thrown out. Anna's husband had now become the black sheep of the family. They had to shift for themselves. Forever after their descendants would be identified as members of the impoverished side of the Seid family.

They were down and out but also prolific. Eleven children were born, six survived. I have no clue as to how they got to America, but I will forever be grateful for that stroke of luck. Mother was the only one born in America. The town was Brooklyn. The year 1908. Mother's father shoved a pushcart through the streets of New York singing out the mantra that told all within earshot his trade, "The knife sharpener!" A dangerous occupation. We were destined never to meet. He died as a result of a traffic accident on the hurly burly streets of that big city, New York.

The family now consisted of Grandma Anna, four boys, and two girls, Jennie and Rachel. One of the boys, Uncle Harry, worked sewing buttonholes, a skilled trade at the time. He stayed in Brooklyn and raised his family. Jennie moved to California where she prospered in the real estate industry. Anna, her three other sons, and Rachel moved to Detroit, the center of the growing automotive industry. The three brothers left the factory work to others. They chose to concentrate on supplying materials to the growing auto plants. America, Land of Opportunity!

Rachel, the girl who would become my mother, entered school. Here she would receive a basic education. One problem remained. How would she learn the manners of a young woman seeking to elevate her position in society? Her mother was from Europe, she only spoke Polish and Yiddish. Never spoke English. Who would show Rachel how to comport herself, speak the language of those aspiring to improve their social position? The answer lay in motion pictures. It was in films one could see actions that were appropriate and acceptable.

One day a fortuitous example of proper behavior occurred when a classmate of Rachel's called to her from the other side of the street inviting her to join him. This boy was standing in front of a storefront used by Detroit's infamous Purple Gang. The Purple Gang was Jewish and vicious. Detroit belonged to the Purple Gang. Rachel thought if that young man wanted her company he, not she, should cross the street. She called to him, saying if he wanted to speak with her, he'd have to come to her. He complied. Just as he reached Rachel a touring car came speeding down the road with machine guns blazing, breaking the storefront's plate glass, and killing the gangsters seated inside. This was a "save" in matters of life and death never to be forgotten by either teenager. It also ensured my future. This was years before the terms Mafia and Organized Crime were common. The Purple Gang used to row boats across the Detroit River smuggling booze. Hollywood has long sold the world on the idea that most "mobsters" were "Italian or Sicilians," but this is not the case. The leader of the Purple Gang was Detroit mobster Abe Bernstein.

My dad was probably the only Jew shoveling coal on Great Lakes freighters. I think of Lou, a tough, streetwise kid with moxie. He took no lip from anyone. No way! He never drank but did begin to smoke at the age of 10. Entertainment meant playing poker, pinochle, or pool. When they sing that phrase, "Tote that bar, lift that bale!" I'd add "never touch a drop, never land in jail." To top it off he was a gamblin' man. When his ship dropped anchor at the port of Detroit he did what any young sailor would do. Lou went ashore looking for a girl. It was 1923. In the Detroit area of those days every ethnic group lived in their own enclave. Hungarians in Del Ray, Poles in Hamtramck, African Americans in Paradise Valley, the Irish in Corktown, and Jews in their Ghetto. Dad found that Jewish quarter and the girl, Rachel, a raven-haired beauty all of 16. They fell in love and were married. He never went back to sea. That's a sailor's story.

My sister, Harriet, was born in Detroit the next year.

I JOIN THE CAST

Early years in the South Bronx.

Always Harriet's little brother.

I made my entrance on Nov. 22, 1926, and what a great ride it's been. At the age of two and a half I took my parents, sister Harriet, and Grandma to a tenement in the South Bronx.

Our tenement was a fifth-floor walkup, no elevator, probably built in the 1880s. Mom's wash would be drying on a line hung between a pole and our window. There weren't enough beds, so I slept with my Grandma Anna until I was 8. Though she never smoked she'd collect cigarette butts to give tobacco to old men who couldn't afford to buy their own. Marilyn, my younger sister, was born in New York.

When the City of New York began to push subway lines into the area at the beginning of the 20th century, the Bronx transformed into a city of its own. The Grand Concourse, a street that was based on the model of the Champs-Elysées in Paris, was opened in 1909. Grand Concourse initiated a housing boom, especially among Jewish and Italian families who were fleeing from the crowded life in Manhattan. The Bronx of the 1920s, '30s and '40s became a staging ground for the American Dream, home to 1.5 million people. But living in a tenement meant sharing two bathrooms on each floor and limited hot water among other inconveniences.

What was it like for a Jewish boy growing up in the Bronx in the 1930s? No antisemitism here. No discrimination. However, grocers did have a problem. The Orthodox rabbis wanted Jews to strictly adhere to the religious Laws. Grocers found it difficult to sell only kosher food and make a living. The old-world rabbis taught us to denounce our grocer as "a bad man" for selling

Jell-O and other such foods in his small store. This was during the depths of the depression, and I knew my father's friend, the grocer, was not the devil. Perhaps it was attitudes like these that began to turn me against Orthodoxy.

We Jews who lived in the South Bronx had little money and couldn't afford to pay for membership in a large, or in some cases, any religious congregation. Storefront synagogues abounded in the South Bronx. Right across the street from our apartment was a tiny storefront shul, which Jews could attend on the High Holidays for a small donation. I remember my sister Harriet's friend Mildred dressing up in a sheet with a pretty belt during Purim to imitate Queen Esther. How did some families fulfill their religious obligations? My friend's brother had his bar mitzvah at a storefront shul. His parents were so poor that he learned his section of the Torah through an intensive short study after they made a small donation to the Rabbi. In addition, his mother used to send a full course meal every time he went for his lesson.

Shopping in the tenements meant mother wrapping coins in paper, leaning out the fifth-floor window and shouting instructions to me in the street below. She was telling me what to buy from the corner store. Of course for insurance, she wrote that shopping list on the paper before tossing it to me.

Playtime after school was great. I was learning to play stickball with friends in the street. Our bat was just a stick that had once been the handle of a broom. Today, while researching the New York Times historical photos of New York I found a wonderful shot of kids playing stickball on the streets of New York in 1935. I could have been one of those boys of the Bronx. All the kids talked about Hank Greenberg, (Hyman Greenberg) who had also played stickball growing up in the Bronx. Imagine, after years of using a narrow stick to hit that ball he now had what must have seemed like a tree, a real baseball bat to meet the ball. No wonder he hit 58 home runs in 1938!

We heard he turned down playing for the New York Yankees. Didn't know why until years later. Seems he had "sechel" a Yiddish word for brains. Rather than compete against Lou Gehrig for the opportunity to play first base he signed with the Detroit Tigers. Greenberg faced antisemitism in the ballpark, at home, and on the road. He'd attended New York University for a year before signing with the Tigers. Hammerin' Hank was one of the most dominant players of his time, one of baseball's premier power hitters. And in 1934, because his faith forbade playing on a Jewish holiday, baseball great Hank Greenberg was attending services at the Shaarey Zedek synagogue in Detroit. He had been scheduled to play in a key game of the American League pennant race but it was Yom Kippur. So instead of playing in that important game he attended the synagogue. The congregation gave him a standing ovation.

Yes! Life is strange and mysterious. Thirty years later, in 1962, I would participate in the Cornerstone Laying Ceremony of the present Shaarey Zedek house of worship. This Detroit-area Jewish Conservative congregation was building a new synagogue. Their senior Rabbi, Morris Adler, asked me to join them. I was to accompany the participating celebrants and using a microphone, describe the consecration ceremony of the laying of the cornerstone. Large speakers would carry my commentary to congregants seated in folding chairs in the area, which would ultimately be the sanctuary. Who could have foreseen the tragic events destined to occur four years hence? It was Shabbat morning Feb. 12, 1966, the anniversary of President Lincoln's birthday. Rabbi Adler had just finished delivering the Lincoln Day sermon when a deranged youth shot and killed him. The youth then killed himself.

Neither of my parents had more than a sixth or seventh grade education. There were many reasons for the lack of more formal education. For sure, life had taken over. By the time I was 3 the Great Depression was in full swing. But Dad was lucky. He got a job washing taxis. It was a large fleet and a steady job. The combination of his height, 5 feet 5 inches, and his history of living on the streets, led to the next rung on the ladder of life. Remember, Dad was a tough kid. At work a big Swede taunted, teased, and challenged him. The response included a bucket of water Dad dumped on the Swede's head. Lou then proceeded to beat him into submission. Marty Radnor, owner of the company, took immediate action. He had two choices: fire Lou or elevate him. The second seemed the most productive. So Dad became the night manager of the fleet. He had a really good job for the first time and at the height of the depression. Now we could move down to the first floor of that tenement. In this case progress was down not up.

My first experience at school was a bit unusual. "This boy is too smart for kindergarten," the teacher said. "Put Shelby into the first grade." So much for determining a child's mental capacity. They'd mistaken daydreaming for thinking. The result? I had to spend two terms in the first grade!

While swimming in the East River at the age of 7, I attempted to get out of the water by grabbing a log. My understanding of physics hasn't improved much since then. That log just kept turning and I was getting exhausted. A black man saw what was happening, ran over and got as wet as I was in the process of extricating that little boy from the dangerous East River. I characterize that event as a stroke of luck, a never-ending series of lucky breaks. They continue to appear and reappear throughout my life.

On another occasion I joined a group of youngsters entering a building on Southern Boulevard. Unaware of their mission, I soon discovered the group's intentions. This building had an underground bowling alley. The kids stood at the head of the stairs taunting and teasing the black maintenance man below. He came charging up the stairs. They all took off running down the street. I saw no reason to leave. They ran, I stayed and waited. This was the beginning of a great relationship. This kindly old man invited me to send a woman's bowling ball down the alley, select a candy bar from a nearby glass case, and suggested I visit whenever I should choose. I can't remember our conversations with any details but suspect we talked about what it was like being a black man in that tough New York environment.

As a fourth-grade student I attended PS 62 on Fox Street in the Bronx. The name of the school was Inocensio Casanova. How's that for coincidence? That's my name! Casanova = Newhouse. And it was here that romance entered my life. I was attracted to a beautiful classmate, Shirley Margolis. Even at the age of 9 I was aware of the appropriate action under these circumstances. A gift would demonstrate my desire to please the object of my affections. I was bold enough to ask my friend at the bowling alley for help. Together, he and I walked down Southern Boulevard to a jewelry store. I pointed at something on display. He told me he couldn't get that, but he'd find something she'd like. Several days later my friend produced an expensive looking box of chocolates. All of this at the height of the depression. I took that box to school. Shirley was overwhelmed by the gift.

The next day her mother appeared at our apartment carrying that box. She wanted to know where I'd stolen it. This development was great! I'd given the gift and got to eat it too! I couldn't know that some 40 years later I'd be reminded of this series of events. Reminded of my first encounter with affairs of the heart.

My big break came in the fourth grade. It wasn't Broadway, but it set the stage for what would become my life's work: radio, television, and film. I played the part of an elephant in a school play. My trunk was a long roll of folded paper attached to my nose. The kids loved it! I knew then and there what I wanted to do the rest of my life. I needed an audience! From that moment on I focused on preparing myself for an acting career. I often locked myself in a room and would read aloud for hours to improve my speech, attempting to lose that New York accent.

The New York school system was outstanding. I'll always be grateful for those teachers who took an interest in us. I'll also thank the librarians who broke the rules, permitted me to check out books from the adult section of the library. They knew I couldn't understand them, but those books were an introduction to a universe I was just beginning to explore.

While at school in the Bronx our class visited the American Museum of Natural History on Manhattan's Upper West Side. I was fascinated by the display of meteorites. Imagine! We were told these rocks or huge stones had fallen hundreds of thousands of miles from other planets or stars in the sky. I'm certain my lifelong interest in things scientific dated from that field trip.

We were introduced to classical music by listening to the "NBC Music Appreciation Hour." It was produced by Walter Damrosch, a composer, conductor, educator, and music consultant to the National Broadcasting Company as well as an early radio pioneer. We learned the melodies of classical compositions by memorizing lyrics that gave us the name of the composition, the composer, and something about the music. I still remember singing "Humoresque a lullaby black written by a man named Dvorak" and "Barcarole from Tales of Hoffman written by Offenbach." The entire student body would assemble in our auditorium to listen to the broadcast. Then we'd take a test.

When our family returned to Detroit, I entered the fifth grade. The teacher was introducing her students to classical music. Yes, she was amazed that this kid from the Bronx with the unbelievable accent was acquainted with many of the compositions.

My social studies teacher in intermediate school gave our class the following assignment. Prepare an essay on any country of your choosing, any country in the world. Include all major facts about that nation and be sure to cover imports and exports. I selected Tibet, a country that at that time had neither. I'm sure my teacher thought I'd pulled a fast one, but she was a good sport.

My essay was the first to be turned in. Classmates couldn't figure out how I was able to complete the assignment so quickly. I'd been reading about Tibet. Found it very interesting. Particularly how the Dalai Lama, the spiritual leader of the Tibetan people, was chosen. The Dalai Lama was known as the embodiment of an ideal of Tibetan values and a cornerstone of Tibetan identity and culture. After a Dalai Lama dies a search begins for a successor, a "soul child" who has fulfilled prophecies, whose body shows certain signs that he's received the spirit of the departed Dalai Lama. Senior monks carry out the search. After experiencing a vision while sitting beside a divine lake they travel the countryside on horseback searching villages for boys precocious in their spiritual attunement. Finally, one is chosen. I always found it fascinating how different societies support myths and beliefs that make it easier to bear our burdens as we journey through the sometimes tragic and difficult stages of our lives.

Here is an important Buddhist's prayer or mantra chant. Om Mani Padme Hum. The entire truth about the nature of suffering and the many ways of removing its causes is said to be contained in these six syllables. Om Mani Padme Hum. All hail the jewel in the lotus. Activities of the current Dalai Lama are frequently reported and supported by worldwide media. He's a distinguished well-respected world leader. Unfortunately, Tibet is now controlled by China. Sadly, efforts to free these people are not supported.

Om Mani Padme Hum. I was 12 when my beloved grandmother Anna became blind, she could no longer see. Anna was moved to a Jewish old folk's home. Then tragedy struck. She died two years later. I was devastated. How could God do such a thing? Take my wonderful sweet dearest companion. She'd never harmed anyone. Just loved us all. No one was able to provide an answer to this question. Om Mani Padme Hum. Though still a boy the word agnostic began to take on real significance. I suspect my readings and studies provided an important step in the process of my choosing agnosticism as my mantra.

Dad never had it easy. But I believe one of the jobs he worked at for a long time enabled him to live to be 86 at a time when the average man of his generation died at 47! They called it Industrial Insurance. Folks would buy a life insurance policy and pay 25 cents a week. That was the premium. Dad was the collector. He'd walk day after day picking up those payments from folks poor as could be. I'm convinced it was that walking, that daily exercise that kept him in good health for so long. The insurance company Dad worked for moved our family from Detroit to Columbus, Ohio where I was enrolled in the eighth grade. Here the intense football rivalry between North and South high schools was the only topic of conversation. Academic subjects didn't exist. Because I'd been a Boy Scout in Detroit I looked for the nearest troop. They met in a church several blocks from our house. When the men in charge of the troop learned I was Jewish I was told I'd have to wait until their next meeting to find out whether I could become a member. I've always been grateful for their decision. When I returned for the next meeting, I learned I could join the troop. Now that we lived in our first house and not an apartment as in Detroit, we could have a pet. Dad brought home a small white dog. We became fast friends. Now I knew heaven was real!

As I approached my 13th birthday, I eagerly looked forward to my Bar Mitzvah, the traditional Jewish ceremony signifying the transformation from youth to manhood. I'm certain my grandfather, who was president of his synagogue in Pennsylvania was looking forward to hearing of the event. The phrase generation to generation has significant weight within Jewish culture. I'd been attending Hebrew School and this would be the culmination of those studies. Another boy in the class was also 13 and I'd been told we would both participate in the ceremony at the synagogue. Instead, that Saturday morning I was asked to sit with members of the congregation while the other young man read from the Torah. I couldn't believe it! What would this mean if I were to go through life never having had a Bar Mitzvah? Since we'd never been able to afford to pay for my religious schooling in Columbus, I concluded that was the reason I'd been excluded from the ceremony. I walked home crying. It was only at the advanced age of 85 that I learned the Bar Mitzvah ceremony was only traditional, not required. Having attained the age of 13 years and one day, ceremony or not, I'd attained manhood. I was a Jewish man.

I don't know the details, but Dad's job must have disappeared. We had to leave our house. Our family left Columbus in the dead of night. I've got to believe there were some merchants whose bills were never paid. While still in the city, Dad pulled over and asked me to take my little dog, put him on a street corner and leave him. I asked, "What will happen to him?" "He'll be picked up. That's for sure. Look at how cute he is." That event proved a 13-year-old could learn several things from a small white dog. Yes, heaven was real. But so was Hell.

THE TEEN YEARS

Original Cass Technical High School, Detroit, Michigan.

We returned to Detroit in time for me to enter the ninth grade. I attended Cass Technical High School, an unusual institution. Detroit's neighborhood high schools offered two curriculums: college preparatory and non-college. Cass Tech however was a vocational school. All classes were labeled college preparatory, and students had to have attained a certain level of academic excellence just to be accepted. They also had to select a specific vocation in which they must excel while continuing to maintain high grades in their curriculum. As a consequence, more than one-third of the entering freshman class would not graduate from Cass. They'd be returned to their neighborhood school because they couldn't maintain the required grades. Those graduating from Cass invariably went on to college.

Why had I chosen to go to this school? Because Cass had the reputation of having the best drama club in the city and I wanted to be an actor. I was focused, had that fire in the belly. Now I needed the skills. Others sought preparation to be a scientist, physician, engineer, artist or musician. Which department would I enter? A decision had to be made. Since I'd been playing the E-flat upright alto horn while attending intermediate school I was able to select the Music Department as my vocational course of study.

Registration in the Music Department required a student be auditioned. Vocalists sang, instrumentalists played their instrument. I played the French horn for Francis Hellstein. He was very kind and recommended I attend the summer school class for French horn, and he'd audition me again in the fall.

I attended summer school, practiced diligently and then auditioned again. Though I still played poorly I was accepted. Horn players are always in short supply. Here's a good example of the quality of the Cass Tech faculty. The Detroit Symphony Orchestra's first chair French horn player Francis Hellstein had conducted my auditions. He was my teacher.

Permit me to move 50 years into the future to my attendance at a nursing home in Farmington Hills, Michigan. The occasion was a 100th birthday celebration for Michael Bistritsky. He became the director of the Cass Tech Symphony Orchestra while I was a student. Those of us who'd gathered to attend this celebration were asked to relate stories of Mr. Bistritsky's years at Cass. You had to be a musician to fully appreciate the story I told. "When Bistritsky arrived I was playing first horn. His ear was so good in just two months I was moved to second chair." He really was an outstanding musician. Typical of the quality of Cass Tech's faculty.

The opportunity to attend this remarkable school was clearly another stroke of luck. Studying the French horn led to a concern about my wind, physical fitness. Music classes were usually on the sixth floor. Our rehearsals and concerts took place in the practice rooms and auditorium on the main floor. I rarely used our school elevators but ran up and down those school steps. Today I'm benefiting from those exercises.

The school had a long-established procedure for selecting a professional actor to play the leading role in the senior play. This year an actor had been engaged but was no longer available since a professional company now wanted him to play a part in their production. Having to hire a freshman just about killed Mr. Belcher, the faculty advisor. As I appeared to be the best available performer, I got the part. More important was the fact that Phyllis McCreedy, an Art Department student, was cast opposite me. She was a junior and beautiful. She was a year ahead of me and beautiful. She was interesting and beautiful. And we had to do a lot of rehearsing. Not since Shirley Margolis in the fourth grade had I experienced such a rush of hormones or spent such an appreciable amount of time with a member of the opposite sex. To say I was stricken would be to put it mildly. There was no formal dating. But I would take advantage of any opportunity to spend time with Phyllis. The urge to merge was certainly present. I distinctly remember one moment when I said something, used an expression I had never spoken before. This obviously represented a concern I had, but never before addressed. I was unaware of her parents' religious or political views. Though they had met at Albion College, a Methodist school, they were not practicing Christians and were deeply involved in liberal political movements. This day we were walking across the street and I said, "You know, I'm a Hebrew?" Where did that come from? Her response was a simple, "Yes."

Those early high school years were intense. In addition to my studies, I experienced several work assignments after school. I was hired as an elevator operator. This required my joining a union. The fee was all of $25. The location? The 10-story Lawyers Building. It had two hand-operated elevators and was located at 137 Cadillac Square in downtown Detroit. I worked as a shoe salesman in a downtown store marketing ladies' footwear. This proved to be an experience preparing me for a similar job years later at Saks Fifth Avenue in Beverly Hills, California. During my senior year I worked the night shift as a staff announcer at WJLB, a Detroit radio station. I earned $32.50 a week plus $25 in fees. The station signed off at 1 a.m.! I was undoubtedly the only student taking a taxi to school so I could get more sleep. The station's announcing staff consisted of two women and this high school senior. That employee profile was the result of the absence of millions of men engaged in something called World War II.

When I joined the staff WJLB was primarily a foreign language station. They aired the Polish American hour, Greek American hour, Italian American hour, French American hour, even the Yiddish American hour! It was a great opportunity to learn key phrases in all those languages. My night shift at the station included "The Interracial Goodwill Hour," a 10 p.m. to midnight program Monday through Friday. Edward A. Baker, an African American advertising executive bought the time. He'd cut stories out of newspapers like the Michigan Chronicle, Chicago Defender, Miami Weekly and while I was still reading other copy, he'd hand these news stories to me to read ... cold! What a wonderful opportunity and training ground for all that was ahead of me in radio.

Due to a dispute between recording companies and the national musicians' union there was a two-year period during which no records were produced. As a consequence, many musicians took to the road, performing live at venues across the country. Bill Randle, host of "Strictly Jive" on WJLB produced a Jazz Concert at the Detroit Institute of Arts. It was billed as, "The First Jazz Concert in Detroit." Coleman Hawkins, renowned tenor sax man and Herb Jeffries, Duke Ellington's vocalist were featured. This concert was historic. Because Randle had to be out front selling tickets and collecting cash, he asked me to be the concert's Master of Ceremonies. The pay? $90! Yes! I was 17.

Not everything had an upside. Allied Youth, an organization promoting sobriety, held an annual oratorical essay contest for ninth-grade students. This organization was convinced all teenagers needed to be alerted to the dangers of alcohol and drugs in the lives of young people. In 1941 the essay title was, "Alcohol as a Problem in a War-Torn World." I won the School, District and City contests. Henry Ford had always attended the annual Allied Youth dinner in the Dearborn Inn. Mr. Ford would present the loving cup to the winning student. This year he chose not to appear. Why? Henry Ford was an antisemite. Typical of his numerous public comments concerning Jews was this one: "I'll take my factory down brick by brick before I'll let any of those Jew speculators get stock in the company." When Henry discovered I was Jewish my fate was sealed. The loving cup would be presented by someone else. My parents understood what was happening though I didn't.

Seventeen years later I got even. The car gods in automotive heaven arranged a response to Henry's dismissal of 14-year-old Shelby Newhouse. The event concerned Edsel, Henry Ford's son. He was an excellent example of the seed falling far, far from the tree. Edsel was a Renaissance man, literate, lover of the arts. In fact, he was Chairman of the Detroit Institute of Arts. His father, president of the Ford Motor Company, was not interested in the world of art or literature. The payback location was Detroit's 1958 International Auto Show. It was the introduction of the Edsel! Automotive writers dubbed it the greatest automotive lemon of all time. No. It was not well received. This car, named after Henry's son, was presented to the world by an experienced narrator hired to introduce the vehicle. Extol the virtues of the new Edsel! You guessed it. I won the toss!

I was now 31 years old and the irony of what was happening did not escape me. Yours truly presented this all-time loser, Ford's Edsel. What would his old man, Henry, have thought of this? I was also given the honor of introducing it at the Chicago and New York International Auto Shows. I was the same kid Henry refused to meet. And in a manner of speaking though it may seem Shakespearean, for that boy who almost met Henry, this was vengeance. Henry eat your heart out!

DISCRIMINATION ON ALL FRONTS

```
                GROSSE POINTE PROPERTY OWNERS ASSOCIATION

NOTE TO INVESTIGATOR:
    GIVE INFORMATION ONLY WHERE INDICATED BY ASTERISKS(*).

NOTE TO COMMITTEE MEMBERS:
    PLEASE READ SECTION C AND SECTION D (ADDITIONAL INFORMATION ITEMS AND THE NARRA-
    TIVE) BEFORE GRADING.

                                        DATE _____

*MR. _____ (COMPLETE NAME)

*MRS. _____ (COMPLETE NAME)

*RESIDENCE ADDRESS _____

*BUSINESS ADDRESS _____

SECTION A.    IS FAMILY AMERICAN? _____ AMERICANIZED? _____

*  (1) WHAT DESCENT.  MR.? _____ MRS.? _____     7

*  (2) AMERICAN BORN.  MR.? _____ MRS.? _____
                                                                     7
        IF NOT, HOW LONG IN U.S.A.?  MR.? _____ MRS.? _____

    (3) IS WAY OF LIVING AMERICAN? _____

*       (A) WHAT IS HIS OCCUPATIONS? _____         4

            TYPICAL OF HIS OWN RACE? _____

*       (B) ARE HIS FRIENDS PREDOMINANTLY AMERICAN OR OTHERWISE?  SPECIFY   14
            TYPE _____

    (4) APPEARANCE:

*       MR.  SWARTHY   VERY ____ MEDIUM ____ SLIGHTLY ____ NOT AT ALL ____
                                                                            6
*       MRS. SWARTHY   VERY ____ MEDIUM ____ SLIGHTLY ____ NOT AT ALL ____

    (5) ACCENT:

*       MR.  PRONOUNCED _____ MEDIUM ____ SLIGHT _____ NONE _____
                                                                            6
*       MRS. PRONOUNCED _____ MEDIUM ____ SLIGHT _____ NONE _____

    (6) NAMES TYPICALLY AMERICAN?  MR. _____ MRS. _____
                                                                            3
        TYPICAL OF OWN RACE?       MR. _____ MRS. _____

*   (7) AGES AND NUMBER OF PERSONS IN FAMILY _____
        _____         3
        _____
        _____ TOTAL   50

*   (8) WHAT PERSONS (IF ANY) OTHER THAN THE SUBJECT AND CHILDREN;

*       (A) OCCUPY PRESENT RESIDENCE? _____    DO
            _____      NOT
```

19

Of course, discrimination against minorities was commonplace, part of the culture. The Grosse Pointe Property Owners Association document demonstrates how profiling of ethnicity was prevalent in the 1940s. It was not unusual to see signs advertising available apartments using the language "Dogs and Jews Not Allowed!"

These sentiments were not restricted to Grosse Pointe. Lily-white Dearborn is another case in point. Dearborn and Mayor Orville Hubbard. He was the well-known symbol of suburban America's resistance to racial integration. Hubbard became the most famous segregationist north of the Mason-Dixon line. His motto? "Keep Dearborn clean." That reference extended to Jews or any "Other." Purportedly he once examined the bullet-riddled body of a black man and called it an open-and-shut case of suicide. His tenure? 1942 to 1978.

Detroit was a segregated community. In the 1920s the Ku Klux Clan, an organization committed to white supremacy, had established a strong presence in our city. By the 1940s many African Americans had moved from their homes in the South to northern cities. They were needed to work in war plants where the Clan had already established itself. They were not welcomed and received no preparation for the different culture they would find.

We were in the midst of World War II. Recruiters toured the South convincing both blacks and whites to head north with promises of high wages in the new war factories. Arrivals came in such numbers that it was impossible to house them all. Blacks who believed they were heading to a promised land found a northern bigotry every bit as pervasive and virulent as what they thought they had left behind in the Deep South. And southern whites brought their own traditional prejudices with them as both races migrated northward. Detroit's population had grown by 350 thousand people since the war began. Times were tough for all, but for the black community, times were even tougher. Blacks were excluded from all public housing except the Brewster projects. In addition to discrimination in public accommodations police also confronted them with unfair treatment. Even our military was segregated.

White communities militantly guarded the dividing lines imposed by segregation throughout Detroit's history. The city's two hundred thousand black residents were now crammed into the East Side. Defense industries with high wages and very little available housing had recently hired 50 thousand blacks. Other new arrivals included three hundred thousand whites, mostly from rural Appalachia. Tensions between the two groups were escalating.

On June 20, 1943, my friend and neighbor Larry and I spent the day canoeing on Belle Isle. It was a beautiful Sunday. Late that afternoon as we approached the foot of the bridge to board our Jefferson Avenue bus for the ride back home, we saw a crowd and several police cars. They'd just thrown a black youth into one car. We overheard people talking of a rumor. A black mother and baby had been tossed off the bridge. Wow! We ran, got on a bus, and took off for home. I later learned that in a neighborhood where southern whites lived a different rumor was making the rounds; blacks had raped and murdered a white woman on the Belle Isle Bridge. Detroit was a tinderbox, ready to explode. Guess what? I'd been present at the start of the historic 1943 race riot.

My father's insurance collection route was in Paradise Valley. This was a 60-block area in Detroit where African Americans lived, many without indoor plumbing, paying two to three times higher rent than white families with similar facilities in white districts. Yet, this ghetto was called Paradise Valley. That morning just as Dad got out of his car several black men ran toward him. A woman shouted, "You leave Mr. Newhouse alone! He's all right!" She told Dad he'd better get home. There was trouble in the city!

It had now reached a fever pitch. Stores were looted and buildings burned. Most of these were in black neighborhoods, the oldest and poorest in Detroit. Clashes soon escalated to the point where black and white mobs were assaulting one another. Both sides encouraged others to join in the riots with false claims that one of their own was attacked unjustly. By mid-morning, black leaders in the community had asked Mayor Edward Jeffries to call in federal troops to quell the fighting. But it was not until late that evening, when white mobs invaded Paradise Valley, that Jeffries took the necessary steps to get outside help. The U.S. Army had to intervene. I remember seeing Federal troops with automatic weapons in armored cars and jeeps. They were moving down Woodward Avenue and later bivouacked in Grand Circus Park.

Around midnight, a disturbing silence reigned over Detroit. A truce between the city's warring factions was kept by U.S. Army troops. More than six thousand soldiers had been strategically stationed throughout the city. Our town was under armed occupation, virtually shut down. Streets were deserted, schools closed, and Governor Harry Francis Kelly shut down all places of public amusement. Most of the Paradise Valley community feared to leave their homes. Yet spurts of violence still flared up.

As late as Wednesday, white mobs threatened black students leaving their graduation ceremony at Northeastern High School. The graduates had to be escorted home by truckloads of soldiers bearing bayonets. Thirty-four people were killed in the riot. Twenty-four were African Americans. And of the roughly eighteen hundred people who were arrested 85% were black. Out of the approximately 600 injured, black people accounted for more than 75%. It took three days before Federal troops restored order. Thirteen murders remain unsolved. Troops occupied Detroit for six months until President Roosevelt felt it was safe to pull them out in January 1944.

FIVE MONTHS LATER . . .

With Dad in line at the Draft Board.

In the army now.

June 1944 was the date. The event? My Cass Tech graduation. The next week my parents and two sisters moved to California. Since I had both a job and a girlfriend I stayed in Detroit. One of the most difficult things I've ever done was to sit down with Phyllis McCreedy, whom I loved, and her parents. We told them Phyllis was pregnant. We wanted to get married. Phyllis was almost 19. But at 17 I was too young to marry in Michigan and we had to recognize World War II was in progress. There were 15 million men in service. We knew I'd be drafted as soon as I became 18.

Our plan was to marry somewhere and then leave Phyllis with her parents. I'd travel to California, say goodbye to my folks and go into service. We did just that! Executed our plan. Phyllis and I took a train to Cincinnati, Ohio. We then walked across the bridge to Covington, Kentucky, where I believed at the age of 12 you could marry your first cousin.

As we strolled along the street a man approached. His job was to steer couples to his employer. Of course I had no idea whether he worked for a minister, rabbi, justice of the peace or whoever. Another couple sat in the waiting room. There were True Romance magazines to occupy us as we waited our turn. The man who was to perform our marriage was very businesslike. He accepted our money. But from the moment the brief service, the marriage ceremony began, he assumed the most unctuous, religious character imaginable. It appeared Phyllis was crying, and I offered her my handkerchief. As we were leaving after the service, I discovered she'd not been crying, but laughing at this charade.

Tearful goodbyes were said in Michigan, and I was off alone on my new adventure. The journey to California was uneventful. It just so happened Dad and I had to report to the draft board at the same time. We actually stood in line together. The army sergeant with his clip board in hand looked at us, asked if we were father and son and then said to Dad "they won't take you, they'll take him." He was right! Uncle Sam thought I'd make a good infantryman. I was sent to Fort Hood, Texas for basic training.

On her 67th birthday I telephoned my daughter Erin to wish her a happy birthday. She asked did I remember where I was the day she was born. I'd forgotten. But she knew, remembered where I had been and what had happened. I was out in the field at Fort Hood participating in some infantry exercise. Our captain refused to permit me to return to camp to take a phone call. That phone call was from the hospital with the news of her birth. There I was, a young father, in love and married, away at war like millions of other Americans. I was angry with my captain, but in retrospect I realize what he was doing was more significant and important than even that phone call. He was preparing me for combat, how to do my job and save my life.

FIVE MONTHS LATER...

On several occasions I've been the target of antisemitism. But here is an example of the tables being turned for my benefit. During hand-to-hand combat training my false front tooth was knocked out. On returning to our base this private visited the camp dentist. His nametag seemed Jewish so I asked where he lived. "Cleveland" was the answer. I knew where Jews lived in that town. I asked, "Would that be in Shaker Heights?" He paused and then reached for my dog tags on which the word Hebrew had been inscribed. The lieutenant picked up a pad, wrote a note and said, "Give this to Major Bloom upstairs." The major read the note, looked at the tooth, threw it away and said, "Soldier, I'll give you a tooth that will never come out." I spent the next two days in his chair. Forty years later my family dentist had to perform a procedure on that tooth. He asked where this wonderful work had been done. I said, "In the military." "Well, you must have been a field officer, at least a major to get that much gold"! Major, hell! I was just a private.

An on-camera smile. Courtesy of Uncle Sam.

As the war in the European theater ended, my infantry basic training was also ending. The army immediately built simulated Japanese villages. We were given advanced training taking these targets. Though the Japanese were losing, they were by no means ready to surrender. Stephen E. Ambrose, an eminent American historian, describes their situation and battle plan:

> They were ready to fight to the last Japanese. They were training women and children in the use of sharpened bamboo stakes, to meet the Marines at the beach. They were preparing the most elaborate defenses, using what they had learned in Iwo Jima and Okinawa. They had hundreds, perhaps even thousands, of kamikaze planes, hidden in caves or in forests. They had kamikaze powerboats, loaded with explosives, ready to hit the American fleet. They had men trained with explosive backpacks ready to crawl under American tanks. To surrender on American terms would be a humiliation for the Japanese military, who were pledged to fight for the Emperor to the last man. They were ready to sacrifice the whole nation to

preserve their personal honor.

For the Japanese the need to end the war was overwhelming. While they were starving and killing American POWs, mainly fliers who had been shot down over Japan, a thousand or more civilians in the Japanese-held territories in Asia and the offshore islands were dying every day because of Japanese mistreatment. The dropping of atom bombs on Hiroshima and Nagasaki saved my life, the lives of a million Americans and about three million Japanese. So today I say thank you Harry Truman. For your courage and decisiveness and common sense. Thank you, Harry! Our president! A haberdasher with guts! Me? A rifleman with luck!

In September 1941, the nation launched an emergency ship construction program that would involve building, in just three years, the equivalent of more than half of the pre-war merchant ships of the world and the greatest fleet of fighting ships the world had ever seen. Henry J. Kaiser, best known for building the Bay Bridge and the Hoover Dam, pioneered new shipbuilding techniques. Operating four yards in Richmond, CA and three in the Northwest, Kaiser developed methods for prefabricating and mass-producing Liberty Ships. Components were built across the U.S. and transported to shipyards where the vessels could be assembled in record time. During the war, a Liberty Ship could be built in about two weeks at a Kaiser yard. In November 1942, one of Kaiser's Richmond yards built the Liberty Ship Robert E. Peary in four days, 15 hours, and 29 minutes as a publicity stunt. By 1943, three Liberty Ships were being completed each day. More than 2,700 Liberty ships were produced at 19 American shipyards from 1941 to 1945. The speed at which Liberty Ships could be constructed allowed the U.S. to build cargo vessels faster than German U-boats could sink them.

I soon joined 5,000 other infantrymen packed into the Liberty Ship USS General William Weigel. These were men I had never seen before or known before. Black men, white men, educated, uneducated, enlisted soldiers. I was assigned a bunk in the hold. The very bottom of the ship. The GI sleeping above me was about four inches from my nose. Fortunately, I didn't suffer from claustrophobia. We were told our ship was the first one to go directly from the States to Japan since before the war. We sailed through several fields of naval mines. Their locations were identified during surrender negotiations aboard the Battleship Missouri. It was rumored we were slated to be the vanguard of the army of occupation. That meant we'd be assigned to guard duty in the snow and cold of Hokkaido, Japan's northernmost island.

It was early evening when we disembarked somewhere between Tokyo and Yokohama. A strange, peculiar smell permeated the air. For me it will forever be the prime element I will associate with that country. I later learned its source. It's called night soil. They had no man-made fertilizer to help food grow. Their fields, their gardens, were covered with human waste.

When we arrived the women of Japan were wearing many, many layers of clothing, not only because of the weather, but they'd been told we American soldiers were all rapists ready to take advantage of any and every Japanese girl or woman. Reflecting now on the history of their military, the kind of men nurtured by that society, it's easy to see how their women could be sold that bill of goods. After all, it was their sons, their fathers, who perpetrated the horrors of the Rape of Nanking, the Bataan Death March, the use of American prisoners of war for bayonet practice, the beheading of captured flyers. I don't believe their government has made an official apology yet.

As our troop train moved through the night passing the lights of villages this 18-year-old, totally ignorant of Japanese culture, couldn't help but wonder what they were doing that night in those homes. And did they really live in rooms made of rice paper?

All troops either entering the country or leaving for the States were processed through the 4th Replacement Depot at Zama. The military used few euphemisms in those days. The somewhat ominous meaning of "replacement depot" was clear. Fortunately, the shooting was over. Zama had been the West Point of Japan. That rumor on the General Weigel turned out to be true. Four thousand nine hundred ninety-nine infantrymen left Zama for Hokkaido. It was time for my next stroke of luck. I was pulled out. Army records showed during my last year in high school I had worked the night shift as an announcer at a Detroit radio station. I never saw Hokkaido. The army had found in me a talent crucial to the success of its mission. My principal duty was a truly dangerous assignment. I was to read the daily news over the camp's loud speakers. I was attached to the Information and Education Office (I and E) of the 4th Replacement depot, Zama, Japan.

Let me try to recreate what it was like at Zama. The winter of '45 was bitter, really cold, with a wind that cut right through you. About eight of us slept in a large room with windows that almost reached the ceiling, and those windows were about 10 feet high. The only heat came from a small coal stove provided by the U.S. Army Quartermaster Corps. Hard to believe, I know, but there had been a foul-up. A shipload of these stoves had arrived in Japan. Each one with a connection to a section of stovepipe to carry smoke out of the room and building. The stoves had arrived . . . the stove pipes were back in the States. With typical Yankee ingenuity GIs roamed the countryside scrounging for whatever they could find to get that smoke out!

Our army cots were placed in a circle with feet as close to the coal stove as possible. A measure of the cold can be found in how we prepared our cots for the night. First, a layer of newspapers, then an army blanket, followed by your sleeping bag, covered by another blanket if you had it, and topped off by tying the arms of your overcoat to the foot of your cot. Crawl into that sleeping bag, zip up, and dream of home. Of course, compared to GIs sleeping in foxholes this was the Hilton.

If you had a pass and got aboard a train, you'd find the car packed with people wall to wall. At only 5'8" I was still head and shoulders over the average Japanese. As a member of the Army of Occupation I did have a concern that our former enemy could have driven a knife into me and I'd still be standing. But incidents of this type were very rare. Obedience and the herd instinct appeared to be among the controlling factors. Incidentally we were cautioned never to eat Japanese food.

Someone in command at Zama decided a museum showing items describing Japanese culture would help GIs pass the time as they waited to be processed. In the usual army fashion, our I and E lieutenant looked around for the most qualified member of our unit, someone steeped in the history, art, politics, culture of this country to research and assemble artifacts for this museum. I guess the fact that I was an 18-year-old high school graduate who knew virtually nothing about Japan qualified me. I got the assignment. Our commanding general signed a document I was to carry. It gave me permission to enter any home or building in or outside of the camp and to confiscate whatever I deemed appropriate for the museum.

At the risk of destroying my relationship with the General who, of course, didn't even know I existed, I just couldn't go into some poor farmers home and take out one or more of his possessions. I couldn't do it. So instead, I went through every building on the grounds of this West Point of Japan, selected many items, and built the museum.

Our lieutenant was a calm, dignified Mormon from Utah. In an effort to provide opportunities for our troops to relax he decided I was just the man to build a ping-pong table. What a gross misreading of my qualifications or abilities. I did what any French horn player would do. Drew up a list of materials I'd require for the job and presented it to the Quartermaster's shop. This city boy knew a table would require legs on which to place the tabletop. So, in addition to wood for the table I requested a bucket of nails and a hammer. What more could I possibly need? After several hours of nailing the piece of plywood to its four legs I stood back to admire my masterpiece. The troops would have hours of fun testing their skill following the bouncing ball. And did that ball bounce! Whenever it hit the exposed top of a nail not even Einstein could have calculated its trajectory or where it was going to land.

BACK ON THE AIR

It didn't take long to discover Armed Forces Radio. WVTR, Radio Tokyo was the only radio station we GIs could listen to. It was Sept. 12, 1945, they had just moved to Tokyo from the island of Leyte in the Philippines. WVTR was the key station of the 18 Armed Forces Radio Stations in the Pacific. I made the right contact, an interview and audition were arranged, and I took off for the big city. They really must have been short-handed. The clouds parted and they offered to exchange my M1 rifle for a hot microphone. The Zama Replacement Depot couldn't argue with a request from General Douglas MacArthur's Headquarters in Tokyo.

Shelby Z. Newhouse and Jack Faulkner 1945-46

What was Tokyo like? Well, it certainly was too early for any American influence. This was Japan, the real Japan. Our fire-bombing of their capitol had been more than successful. There was rubble everywhere. In the picture of Jack Faulkner and myself, we're standing on the steps of the JOAK building in downtown Tokyo that now housed WVTR our station. That building was a survivor. It stood in downtown Tokyo in good shape. If memory serves me correctly, it was within walking distance of the Emperor's Palace, the Dai-Ichi building that housed General Headquarters and the Supreme Commander for the Allied Powers (SCAP) himself, Emperor MacArthur.

So I joined the WVTR staff, low man on the totem pole. The fact that I was able to move up in seniority quickly had nothing to do with ability, but everything to do with everyone's mad dash to get home, back to the States. People were scrambling to get out. Secretary of War Patterson had decreed the point system would be used to determine when you'd get to return and be discharged. Points were earned for time served overseas. Some of our guys had been away from home three and four years.

Sgt. Hans Conried, our Program Director, was my immediate superior. Hans was a well-known eccentric Hollywood personality and a great guy to work for. Let me tell you where I'd seen him in the States. It was prior to the advent of television. In the 1940s seats in the audience of radio shows were in demand. As a teenager visiting my family in California, I'd been in a radio audience and had seen Hans at work. The year was probably 1942. So, working for him in Tokyo was a real treat.

I can relate a great story about Hans' arrival at the station when it was on the island of Leyte in the Philippines. The staff was baffled, unsure of how to handle him. What could they do with this strange Hollywood character? Finally, the decision was made to let him try the morning show, the wake-up call, spinning records. What they didn't know was that Hans loved classical music. He was also a devoted fan of Gilbert and Sullivan. So the GIs were fed a morning disc jockey show of Beethoven, Brahms, Mozart and "The Pirates of Penzance!" That didn't last long! WVTR was the one and only station GIs could listen to! His show generated a tremendous uproar! What did those GIs want to hear? Music that made them homesick. Tommy Dorsey, Harry James, "Sentimental Journey," Les Brown with Doris Day, Bing Crosby, Frank Sinatra, "My Dreams Are Getting Better All the Time," "It Might as Well Be Spring," Dick Haymes, "There Goes That Song Again," "Temptation," Perry Como. After some head scratching, they did come up with an assignment that fit Hans to a T. He was directed to read the comics to the troops! All that on the island of Leyte. I don't remember Hans ever going on the air in Tokyo. I guess as Program Director he didn't have to. He was also an avid art collector, a genuine connoisseur. I enjoyed watching him sitting on his bed doing yoga exercises.

Armed Forces Radio had no table of organization, so whenever a slot opened making it possible to move to a higher rank that opening went to another outfit. The move to higher rank would have translated to more pay, responsibilities and prestige. We were more than unhappy with this system. It was un-American. When we were again bypassed for an opening in rank, as the station's Chief Announcer, I scheduled myself for the night shift so I could read the sign-off copy. This language was very much as if it were the shutting down of a commercial station back home in the States. Instead of saying, "owned and operated by," we said, "operating under the jurisdiction of." For a solid week I closed the station saying, "operating under the jurisdiction of GENERAL Douglass MacArthur. This is PRIVATE Shelby Newhouse, signing off." This didn't get the desired attention of our officers. It was clear they didn't give a damn. They couldn't have cared less. We never got any feedback from GHQ. But when I flew home on an emergency furlough, I experienced evidence that every GI receiving our signal listened to the station until we signed off the air. We were island hopping, flying from island to island. Before returning to our plane there'd always be the inevitable roll call. When they'd come to my name the entire group would shout out, "That's PRIVATE Newhouse!"

Many of our shows originated from the same studio previously used by the infamous Tokyo Rose. Her sexy programs were designed to make us homesick. I recall a truly memorable broadcast of ours that seemed particularly appropriate for that studio. One of our daily chores was to read the news to stations down the line. We'd read very slowly, repeating every line so the news could be typed or written down by hand and read later by someone at that station. They had no recording capability at the receiving end. On this particular day the assignment fell to an announcer who was suffering from the GI's! In some quarters it's called dysentery. At one point in the broadcast, he made an executive decision. Aware that it had been Tokyo Rose's studio this newsman rose to the occasion. He moved a wastebasket, sat on it, and whenever nature called just turned off the mike.

Years later historians were writing the history of Armed Forces Radio in the Pacific. They found someone who had worked at the station in the '50s and were ready to prepare their material when it was discovered I was still around and had worked at the station a few weeks after it went on the air in 1945. I was asked to prepare a memoir of my experiences. That memoir can be found at this web site: http://www.radioheritage.net/Story33.asp. The following line appears in the memoir:

> We had a marvelous shoulder patch worn just above the Eighth Army insignia. Mine disappeared over the years. I wish I had it now. It was sewed with gold thread against a black background and curved to fit the top of your shoulder.

Carol Lowden, a neighbor of ours, visited the web site and learned about the lost insignia. She was kind enough to research, purchase it and give it to me.

The years 1945-46 were filled with experiences no college could have provided. Among other recollections I wrote of acquiring a beautiful silk painting being displayed by its artist on what had once been the Ginza, Tokyo's Rodeo Drive. Remember, when I was there the Ginza was just rubble. This artist had cleared a small area to display his work and the painting was being held down by broken pieces of concrete. Where did I get the money to buy this piece of art? Every so often our Quartermaster Corps would give each of us two cartons of cigarettes. I've never smoked so I used these as barter. I bought that painting for two cartons.

One of the many emails I received from folks who accessed my memoir was an example of one-upmanship. The author of the email said he'd been in Tokyo when I was there and bought the same painting probably from the same artist. He got his for ONE carton!

Whenever possible I'd buy a gift for Phyllis. It would always be something Japanese she'd never be able to find in the States. Guess what? The real world took over and Phyllis ended up without a single one of those gifts! Our unit's assignments included hosting groups of visitors from the U.S. One morning I was studying a list of visitors and saw the name of a man I knew. Gus Scholle, a Michigan Labor Leader, and dear friend of my father-in-law. These visitors arrived and while chatting with Gus he referred to the brevity of his visit to Japan and his concern that he'd never have the time to be able to find gifts for his wife. I showed him what I'd acquired for Phyllis and sure that I would have plenty of time to find and buy more I sold everything to him. That was a major mistake. I left Japan shortly thereafter on an emergency furlough. For years Phyllis would see everything I'd bought for her either worn by or in the home of Mrs. Scholle! I dreaded those invitations to her dinner parties. Dining on plates intended for Phyllis. Seated beneath a painting chosen for Phyllis. Seeing that beautiful Japanese shawl that should have been worn by Phyllis. There are some things one never lives down. The French term faux pas took on a Japanese inflection.

My Honorable Discharge showed I'd earned four decorations: the Asiatic Pacific Campaign Medal, Army of Occupation Medal, World War II Victory Medal, and Good Conduct Medal. At that rate if I'd only served another six months, I'd have looked like Audie Murphy, the most decorated soldier in World War II.

A CAREER BEGINS

Discharged and back in Detroit I studied radio directing at Wayne University. Our professor was Charles Livingstone, director of the "Lone Ranger" broadcasts. Fran Striker was the writer, and the broadcasts came from WXYZ Detroit studios. I was cast as an actor on several of those radio programs. Playing the Young Parson from the East was my favorite role. There was a total of 2,956 radio broadcasts of "The Lone Ranger." The television series ran from 1949 to 1957. Who will ever forget the cry, "Hi-Ho Silver! Away!" Brace Beemer played the Lone Ranger on the radio shows I worked. Did a great job but played the star role to the hilt! Example: during rehearsal of my first show when it came time for my line, Brace was on one side of the mike, two other actors were on the other side. I approached his side of the mike to create the balance. Not three to one, but two on each side. Brace walked away and stood in a corner. The other actors waved me to their side. No matter how many actors were in the scene Brace always was alone on his side of the mike. A small group of Detroit actors worked these programs for many years. Among them were my friends, Liz Weiss and her husband, Rube.

I don't know how often this occurs to others, but for some unknown reason certain names keep appearing. For example, when I was a student at Cass the boy's counselor was Art Stenius. His brother had played the role of the Lone Ranger under the name of George Seaton. This was early in the radio series. He moved on to Hollywood and later in my story reappears as the writer and director of major films. George tried to help me sell a film script. You probably know the name James Lipton. He was a grade ahead of me at Detroit's Hutchins Intermediate School. Of course, we knew him as Jimmy. For a time he was cast as the Lone Ranger's nephew, Dan Reid. Yes, I almost died of jealousy. For years we saw him on television as the host of "Inside the Actors Studio."

In search of a regular job, I went to work as an announcer at WBCM, the ABC affiliate in Bay City, Michigan. This was a small Midwest Michigan town. Farmer Peet owned the station. I've since learned he was never a farmer. Peet placed the station's studios in Bay City's old Wenonah Hotel. Though it was a farming community the area was also known for its wonderful homes. Michigan's lumber barons had built these mansions. Phyllis, our daughter Erin, and I lived on Water Street. Of course, there was a river running through Bay City. The Saginaw River. What was the effect of living in this rural small-town environment? Remember, I was a product of the urban, so-called sophisticated New York Bronx and Michigan's major city, Detroit. What I discovered was that these were not country bumpkins. They were respectful of veterans, wanted to know what's playing at the movies, how are the kids doing at school, were interested in the Detroit Tiger's baseball standing, what are the state legislators up to? Yes, I was growing up. Our interests and concerns were more alike than different.

In 1947, just one year after landing the Bay City job, I responded to the allure of Hollywood. Phyllis and our daughter Erin rode there in style. They took the Santa Fe Super Chief to be met by my mom and Dad at the train station in Los Angeles. Our limited resources dictated a somewhat different mode of travel for me. With the sum of $25 and my good thumb to carry me across the country I was on my way. I'd vowed not to ask Dad for any money to pay for that trip.

This was my strategy. If I were on the road looking for a ride when the sun went down, I'd set out for the nearest bus station to board a Greyhound bus. That meant I'd spend a small sum riding through the night sleeping, but still moving west. My routine changed when I was picked up in Amarillo, Texas. He was a professional gambler driving old Route 66 on his way to Las Vegas. Though Vegas meant veering slightly off course this'd be about a 1,400-mile ride. Our deal was simple. I'd help him drive. We got to Vegas and went our separate ways. He to the tables where the action was, I to the end of town where there was no action.

There I was at the edge of the desert wearing my wrinkled army uniform, carrying a duffle bag, looking bedraggled and needing a shave. What an unlikely subject to be picked up. Hours later, after not a single car had stopped to even ask where I was headed, I set out to find work. I hoped to earn a few dollars and get on that Greyhound bus again. The Flamingo casino had just opened. Thinking I could possibly get a job washing dishes I carried my duffle bag into the opulence of the strip's newest addition and asked about work. They wouldn't hire me to shine shoes let alone get my hands on their dishes. By midnight I had to give in, admit defeat, swallow my pride, wire Dad for $10 and board my chariot, the Greyhound bus, to reunite with my family.

I was now at the center of the entertainment world, the West Coast, Hollywood! They weren't ready for me. Like all aspiring actors I did get an agent. One of the auditions I attended taught me a basic truth. Casting is to type. Unless you're among the top earners in the business, you must look the part or forget it.

Broadly speaking, there are two types of actors. One assumes the role completely. Becomes the character. The other always plays himself. Example? My agent sent me to an audition. When my turn came to meet the director and producer, they just looked at me and said "next." I'd been dismissed.

I asked, "Don't I even get a chance to read the part?"
One said, "You don't fit the character."
"How did they know?" I asked.
The answer, "It's the role of a Jewish poet."
I cried out, "But I am Jewish!"

That prompted gales of laughter. I'm sure they thought this kid would say anything to get the part.

One sunny afternoon two old men were at the beach exchanging stories about their sons. My dad was proudly describing my achievement as a radio announcer at the age of 17 while still in high school. Then his companion spoke of his son, Jerry. His professional name was Jerome Lawrence. He and his partner were writing and producing a radio series, "My Favorite Story." With that connection and my AFRA union card (American Federation of Radio Artists) I was able to get work! These pros were terrific! Several years later Jerome Lawrence and Robert Lee wrote one of the best stage plays ever to reach Broadway, "Inherit the Wind." It was later turned into one of the most successful films of all time.

Between occasional radio shows with Jack Webb (Sgt. Friday), Ed Begley, and others I needed a steady job. Once again it was Dad paving the way. Fortunately, he knew someone at the Palace, a gambling casino on the beach in Venice. Members of an organized crime family ran this California Palace. Working there gave me an opportunity to observe the way these characters operate and how their minds work. Here's a true story. One of the employees stole $5,000 and disappeared. Gee! Everyone thought he'd be found, caught, and killed. They did find him in Mexico, but guess what? They didn't kill him. He wasn't even punished. Instead, they brought him back and gave him a better job. They now had the most loyal employee in the house. He didn't dare step out of line. And they took a portion of each paycheck to get their stolen cash back. They are essentially businessmen. After two years the corrupt politician who had made the Palace Casino possible experienced his inevitable fate. He was defeated at the polls. Immediately, police padlocked our den of iniquity.

The experience of working at the casino provided the basis for a musical Phyllis and I wrote. One of the principal plot lines of our story was the expectation the casino thief would be found and killed. And indeed, that might have been his fictional fate, but the great twist in our story came from the real world of Organized Crime. The bottom line, what was most important, was how to get their stolen money back. When our script was completed, we sent a copy of "Gamblin' Man" to my high school teacher Art Stenius in Detroit. Remember, I knew of his Hollywood connections through his brother George. By now, George had written and directed major films such as "Miracle on 34th Street" which had won three Oscars, including one for George as Best Writing,

Screenplay. Phyllis and I hoped he might be able to walk our musical through that feature film market. Several months later George Seaton notified us that our story "Gamblin' Man" was under consideration for purchase by Frank Sinatra. Yes, we walked on clouds for months. Our dreams of what might have been were shattered when we learned Sinatra had ultimately chosen to pass on our project.

A second disappointment occurred with the release of the box office sensation "Elmer Gantry" starring Burt Lancaster and Jean Simmons. That film won three Oscars. Its storyline was a dead ringer, a virtual parallel to another project we submitted. Our male lead was a drunken dishonest street preacher. He was a con man involved with a female evangelist. We had high hopes for this dramatic story line, but the opening of "Elmer Gantry" killed that possibility.

The next year I worked at a number of jobs, including one that provided me with a great opening line whenever I subsequently gave a talk to women's groups. "Would you like to shake the hand that held the foot of Elizabeth Taylor"? True! I was working in the shoe salon at Saks Fifth Avenue on Wilshire Boulevard. This beautiful young actress came in with a girl friend and I was the lucky salesman whose turn it was to wait on them. Liz Taylor bought two pairs of shiny black patent leather Mary Janes for herself and her girlfriend.

At one point Phyllis and I lived with my parents. Their home was in a very pleasant neighborhood in Santa Monica. Not upscale, but middle class. At that time, I was driving a 1935 Packard with a rumble seat. It was a beast, but I thought it was beautiful. Neighbors said that car didn't fit the surroundings. They complained when I parked in front of Dad's home. So I began parking several blocks away and would walk home.

To augment our meager income Phyllis baked cakes. I tried to sell them door to door. This led to an important discovery. Door-to-door sales was not my forte. We ate a lot of cake! One day as Phyllis and I walked our daughter Erin along the Venice beach several women stopped to admire our child. One asked if we were babysitting. We confessed she was our daughter. Their response? "Why you're children yourselves"!

PUTTING DOWN ROOTS
Thank You Detroit News

SHELBY NEWHOUSE
WWJ
AM—FM—TV

Three years in California on short rations motivated a return to Detroit. The very day we got back I learned there was a two-week job opening at Michigan's first television station, the NBC affiliate, WWJ-TV. The Detroit News owned this station and radio station, WWJ. Few are aware that the building housing that radio station was the first structure in the entire world ever designed expressly for broadcasting. The studios are suspended within the building to prevent vibration from street traffic outside.

Life takes many strange, unexpected turns. The following series of events may appear to be fictional, but they are true. The television station, known as Channel 4, had hired a new employee. This lucky announcer had just been married. WWJ-TV was so prestigious it normally wouldn't even audition a 23-year-old. But it was time for another stroke of luck. I was hired to fill in while the newlyweds had a two-week honeymoon. This must have been the mother of all honeymoons. That announcer never returned, never showed up. My two weeks turned into 26 years!

WWJ Radio had a contract with the American Federation of Radio Artists. Their labor agreement didn't cover the new Detroit News television station, WWJ-TV that had recently gone on the air. AFRA had now become AFTRA. As a member of the union, I chose to run for the board of directors. I won and served on that board for 12 years. I take personal pride in relating the following example of the importance of the trade union movement.

Sam's Cut Rate, the largest cut-rate department store in Detroit, chose to sponsor an hour-long television program. This show would be coming from New York. It starred Milton Berle. Auditions were held for the role of the commercial announcer who'd have to deliver five one-minute spots. It was 1950. Neither videotape nor teleprompters were in use yet. The commercials had to be performed live. The announcer could write the copy on cards and pay a stagehand to run those cards along the edge of the camera's lens. Or all of the copy would have to be memorized. I won the audition, memorized and delivered the five spots flawlessly. Remember, our union contract covered radio, but not television. This meant no rates had been established for the work I'd performed. The Detroit News, owners of the station, came up with a fee they thought I'd earned. They chose to pay me $3 for each spot. I'd earned $15!

Some months later I was a member of the AFTRA team negotiating the station's first TV contract. At the first negotiation session Ed Wheeler, Detroit News Director of Radio and Television, opened his presentation by saying the owners had an excellent contract with employees of WWJ, their radio station. Relations were great! Why did they need another contract covering television? We union members caucused, and I related my Sam's commercials experience. After returning to the negotiating table Boaz Siegel, our attorney, told my story. That took the air out of our employer's presentation. In short order we concluded the negotiations with a good and fair contract.

Everything on early television was an experiment. The camera caught many mistakes that must have amused or perplexed our audience. One famous incident occurred when a network announcer lost his concentration, took a deep drag on his cigarette, slowly exhaled, looked at it lovingly and in his most sexy voice announced, "Ahhh . . . that's coffee."

I made my share of mistakes. I managed to break the unbreakable Melmac dinnerware on camera. Today I'd probably have a senior moment, but at age 23, I simply held up the damaged plate so the cameraman could get a good shot of it and said, "If this happens to you take it back. It's guaranteed." That on-the-spot ad lib was clearly a save for all of us! The ad agency executive, the product, the station, and myself. I remain convinced it contributed to my longevity at the station. I characterize it as an insurance policy. All stagehands are a very sophisticated group of reviewers. Pete, working on our show, muttered three words as he crossed the stage and moved past me. Pete said, "That was good." Considering the source, his three words constituted an extraordinary review of the performance that had just occurred.

> The following item appeared in the Detroit News in 1952.
>
> Three-year-old Marc was fascinated by the 'hill' showing in the giant mirror while it was leaning on the floor against the wall. Shelby Newhouse, with parental patience, explained that the carpet looked like a hill due to the angle of the reflection. Retorted his small son, "Well, Daddy. I wish I was inside the mirror so I could slide down that hill."

Years later, as a tough, experienced ironworker building towers, bridges and skyscrapers, Marc could slide down more than hills. Incidentally, the first time my son saw me on television he was five. Marc ran behind the box to see if I was really in there!

Returning to amusing anecdotes occurring in the early delivery of television commercials. A friend of mine had a medical condition and couldn't drink beer. Guess what? He won an audition that required drinking the sponsor's product on camera. It was beer. The sympathetic director arranged for a cut-away shot as the glass was being raised and it worked beautifully during rehearsal. But that night a different crew did the actual show. What the television audience at home or in a tavern saw was the glass being raised to my friend's lips as the cameraman zoomed in for a close-up. The producer did not cut away as planned. Instead, he followed the action. The viewer saw the contents of the glass being poured into a potted plant. I wish I could have been in a bar and seen as well as heard the response to that.

For two years I was the spokesperson for Altes Beer. Two shows a week: the "Michigan Barn Dance" and a program I can't even remember. My friends loved to see me doing those commercials. They knew I neither drank nor liked the smell of beer. As I reflect on television advertising in the '50s, I remember the words of Jam Handy Studio's casting director. I did a lot of freelance work there. She'd say, "Shelby, I cast you in films and on commercials that require someone who looks intelligent." A beautiful example of my being miscast was the "Michigan Barn Dance." I'd be dressed in jeans and a cowboy shirt, sitting on a bale of hay, surrounded by several other bales and demonstrating my love for the great taste of Altes beer. At one point I was the announcer on the longest running show in Detroit, Frieda Barth's "Good Cooking Show." It was sponsored by the Michigan Consolidated Gas Company and ran for six years!

I was also the announcer on "The Arthur Murray Dance Party." Doris Eaton Travis, who owned the Michigan Arthur Murray franchise told the television audience even the announcer could be taught dance steps. So, she and I would do a different dance routine each week. My children thought that was a fraud. They knew their father didn't need dancing lessons. He was already a good dancer. Indeed, they'd been told their mother and I had earned money while in high school dancing at special events like War Bond Drives. Phyllis would wear an evening gown and I'd rent a tux. We performed two numbers, a tango and waltz encore. I still have a picture of myself carrying Phyllis on my shoulder while doing the tango.

Jan. 18, 2010, I googled Doris Eaton Travis when I discovered she was not only the last Ziegfeld Follies girl but WAS STILL DANCING AT THE AGE OF 105! I sent her this email:

> Doris, you are my inspiration! Permit me to test your memory. For a two-year period in the 1960s you and I had many opportunities to dance. Your television show on WWJ-TV was called "The Arthur Murray Dance Party." Each week the announcer was taught a new dance step and routine which he performed with you in his arms. I was that lucky announcer, Shelby Newhouse. Ignorant as I was, I had no idea of your fascinating history. All I knew was that I was being paid to perform with a wonderful and very interesting woman. How lucky can a guy get? Today, as a youngster of 83, I was casually researching the history of several persons with whom I've worked and found your story. Can't tell you how pleased I am to learn about you and your accomplishments. I'll never forget the intersection of our lives. Thank you. Love, Shelby

I learned Doris died in May 2010, in Commerce, Michigan. At the age of 106!

For two years in the early '50s I also did the announcing on Mort Neff's "Michigan Outdoors" until it moved from our NBC affiliate to an ABC station. When Mort would enjoy his annual 10-day vacation for trout fishing in Chile I would take over and do the entire show.

One of the benefits of being employed by the Detroit News stations was the opportunity of developing relationships with extraordinarily talented individuals like Mischa Kotler and his wife Malinka. Mischa was the Detroit Symphony Orchestra's pianist. There's no way to measure such a friendship. Mischa was also on the Detroit News radio and television staffs. To attend parties and other events in his company was wonderful. He often acceded to requests of those present and performed for us. Mischa died at the age of 95.

A PAUSE FOR THE PERSONAL

Together in California. Top: Sister Harriet, husband Bernie, me. Below: Dad, Mother, Niece, Nephew, and Phyllis holding Erin.

A home in Michigan, a growing family.

Kim, Dana, Marc, and Erin enjoying a moment together with their new puppy Sherry.

With Dana, Kim and Marc. They were growing up!

My beautiful Phyllis. Wife and mother of four.

Enjoying the holidays. Marc, Kim, Erin, Dana, Phyllis, and proud father and husband.

A PAUSE FOR THE PERSONAL

This may be a good place to discuss both my 36-year marriage with Phyllis McCreedy and our four children. Since she was not Jewish my father's parents never recovered from my marriage to Phyllis. As a grandson, I continued to be a member of the family, however my children were never recognized. Their names never mentioned. I was deeply saddened having been responsible for my grandparent's pain. Yet I completely understood this to be the result of their experiences in Europe at the hands of non-Jews. They could feel no other way. However, once Grandmother Rose died my grandfather relented and did accept our children. Perhaps the most constant element in life is change. There will be change. Not only in the weather, but virtually everything. Count on it. Even such a small thing as my son Dana's name. At the time of his birth the name Dana was typically given to a male. Today, many women are called Dana.

Phyllis' grandmother was a minister's wife. Her grandfather led the congregation of Detroit's Metropolitan United Methodist Church. Their membership peaked at 7,300 in 1943. After his death her grandmother lived in a home for retired ministers and their wives. On one occasion she was kind enough to give me a tour of the facility. As we walked down one of the halls she revealed how broadminded this denomination had become. Aware that I am Jewish I'm certain she was trying to make me comfortable when she said, "You know we now have Catholics here." I answered, "Is that right?" "Yes!" she said, "They work in the kitchen." I'm not sure how I was able to do it, but I did not laugh. Clearly, in her view having Catholics working in the kitchen was a real concession.

One year Phyllis experienced an illness that coincided with a planned vacation visit to my folks in California. The dates couldn't be changed. Her physician would approve the trip only if we took a sleeping car on the train. As we approached a stop in Cheyenne, Wyoming, Phyllis announced the need to refill one of her medicines. The railroad personnel assured me there'd be plenty of time to get what we needed at the station's pharmacy. I got off the train, bounded into the station, purchased what Phyllis had asked for and returned in time to see the Santa Fe Super Chief speeding off into the distance with my sick wife and several children on board.

Racing into the station's ticket office I shouted, "Where's the nearest airport?"

In a calm voice the ticket agent said, "You missed the train."

"Yes," I replied. "Can I fly to the next town"?

She said, "They usually take a cab to Laramie. It's only about 50 miles. Cab should be outside."

She was right. There was a cab at the taxi stand.

I ran over and shouted at the relaxed driver behind the wheel, "Laramie, got to get to Laramie, now!"

In a calm voice he said, "You missed the train."

"Yes," I said. "Got a sick wife and kids on board! Can you take me"?

"Yup," he said. "$25 cash . . . up front."

I pulled out the money saying, "Here!"

"Gotta check in first," he said.

"Call in, call in," I demanded!

In a very casual way he answered, "Can't! Got no phone. We'll drive in, takes just a minute."

He drove, I fretted. We arrived and he casually walked into the dispatcher's office. When he came out, he slowly got in the cab saying, "We usually make it. It's uphill all the way." A few minutes later I noticed the road ran parallel to the train tracks. Couldn't see the train, but in a little while we were running alongside.

"Mister," the cabbie said, "I guarantee your wife sees us an' the porter will tell her you're in this cab. Ain't no other reason for us to be on this road, 'ceptin' it's you missed the train."

That's exactly what was happening. The porter was telling Phyllis the same story. We pulled into the Laramie station two minutes before the train arrived.

Our family was growing. We now had Erin Adrian, Marc Lindsey, Dana Ingersoll and Kimball Cameron. Dana's birth was announced to the world and his father on the 11 p.m. Channel 4 television news. I was in the studio ready to introduce the program and do the scheduled Bulova Watch commercials when the control room received a phone call from the hospital announcing Dana's birth. The show was starting so there was no time to give me the news through the studio's audio system. I introduced the newscast and as usual, Dick Westercamp the newsman, appeared on camera to say good evening. He then announced Dana's birth. When they cut to me to do the first commercial I'm told I was grinning like a Cheshire cat. I can just see our obstetrician watching this newscast at home, jumping up and shouting, "I delivered that kid!"

At the age of two our son Dana was crawling across the floor in his grandparents' cottage when he caught the attention of a visitor. The guest was a famous neurologist from the University of Michigan School of Medicine. Talk about a stroke of luck. This physician watched him crawl, noticed what he thought required some attention and suggested we take our son to his doctor. Our pediatrician thought Dana might have a condition called Legg Perthes. That's a softening of the head of the femur at the hip. If left untreated as the femur hardens again it becomes deformed resulting in a severe lifelong limp.

From the pediatrician we moved to the orthopedic specialist. The diagnosis was uncertain, but the conservative approach would be to treat the situation as if it were Legg Perthes. There was no pain associated with this condition, so it was a tough decision for us to make. Dana was sedated and a hip cast put in place. When he awoke, he was immobilized. The cast ran from his hip to his ankle on one leg. His cries at being unable to move were unbearable.

But ultimately the diagnosis did prove to be correct. After 18 months the cast was removed and replaced by a metal brace for another year while the atrophied leg and foot became normal. The success of this treatment could be measured when in the sixth grade Dana won his school's 60-yard dash and citywide long jump competition. I was so elated I searched for the telephone number of the orthopedic physician who had cared for him. I wanted to report his present physical condition and thank him again. When I reached the doctor's wife, I discovered this good man had committed suicide.

In the early '50s, the UAW moved their president Walter Reuther from a home in Detroit to Rochester, Michigan. In order to maintain the integrated neighborhood in which he had lived, Reuther would only sell his home to a Caucasian family. Phyllis and I shared this view and bought the house on Longfellow. Reuther, a very controversial figure, had been attacked and shot in a previous home. So, the doors and all window shades of this beautiful Georgian Colonial were bullet proof. I felt like placing a neon sign on the rooftop announcing, "WALTER DOESN'T LIVE HERE ANYMORE!"

While waiting for the sale to go through we experienced what might have been a serious event. The home we were selling was near the edge of Detroit's city limits. The neighborhood was virtually 100 percent Caucasian. However, our next-door neighbor was the family of an African American Detroit police officer. We told our real estate salesman he could show our home to any potential buyer. One afternoon the house was shown to an African American family. On returning that afternoon we found we'd been vandalized. Someone had broken a basement window, taken our garden hose, inserted it through the window and turned on the water. I called the police and explained what had happened. I not only asked for assistance, but also for a demonstration of police activity to show our neighbors an investigation was underway to find the guilty party. That night I wouldn't let Phyllis and the children stay in the house. They left to spend the night with her parents. I next called Ward, my brother-in-law, and invited him to stay in our home with me. We remained awake all night armed with baseball bats in the event they'd be needed.

The next morning there was still no evidence of any police interest or activity concerning what had happened. I placed a call to Detroit's Chief of

Police and requested a meeting. His office immediately set up a time for this. As I was a well-known member of the media, I'm reasonably certain they thought this was to be some sort of public relations interview. The Chief was surprised when he was confronted with my complaint. By the time I returned home a patrol car with two officers was already stationed in front of the house. Neighbors were questioned. There were no further incidents. We moved into Reuther's home several days later. We only occupied that wonderful Georgian Colonial home for a year. I'd made a serious mistake. We couldn't afford it. To provide heat that winter cost over $100 a month. We next spent a year in Ferndale and then moved to Birmingham, Michigan, to take advantage of their excellent educational system. We lived in Birmingham the next 25 years.

My children benefited from one of the finest school districts in the country. And they still speak of living on the same street with over 40 other youngsters. It seemed like one large playground. An empty lot was next door. This city boy, yours truly, who couldn't tell which end of the hammer to use was determined to build a fort for all the children on the block. Our kids and I drove a truck to Wild Fowl Bay in Michigan's thumb where Phyllis' parents had their cottage. We picked up a load of sections of bark from large trees. These innocent strips of wood spent the next few years as the exterior of a frontier fort in Birmingham, Michigan.

Life in Birmingham included living with our wonderful Norwegian elkhound, Shana. She was a wanderer, and we occasionally received a call from the pharmacy uptown. Shana would walk through their door to sit next to the day's supply of the Detroit News. We're certain she could have read the news, but she seemed to be satisfied just watching customers retrieve their paper. On one occasion as I was driving through town looking for Shana I spotted her playing several blocks from home in Shane Park. I pulled over, opened the passenger door, and called to her. She came running, jumped in, and sat on the seat. Then she turned, stared at me for a moment, jumped out and ran straight home! It was clear she'd realized the error of her ways.

In the early '50s and '60s Phyllis and I belonged to a small book club. The group numbered no more than eight or nine friends at any time. Arthur Nesse and his wife Dorothy were members. Who was Art? His 37-year business career at Ford Motor Company featured a leadership role in computer applications. His official title was Manager of Computer Planning and Control.

Art's early history is fascinating. He was born in 1922 in the province of Henan, Central China, the son of missionary parents. He attended the American School at Kikungshan but moved frequently. These moves were dictated by wars and revolutions that made the school's primary site on Ki Kung Shan (Jigong Shan mountain or Rooster Mountain in English) unsafe. In 1993 a granite memorial was erected to commemorate the many years of

A PAUSE FOR THE PERSONAL

American presence on Jigong, the ASK school, and the missionaries buried in a cemetery there. Art and I devoted considerable time to the development of a potential film documentary about this "Moongate" memorial. Sadly, we were unable to raise the necessary funds for a production. What a great trip that would have been!

Over the years folks dropped away from our small club. Members moved on as life took over. But the Nesses continued to forward annual Christmas letters. Their most recent missal was inspirational. Art had turned 90 and was still playing tennis and golf. I wondered if the fact that his son was the head of the world-famous Mayo Clinic was in any way responsible.

In our search for a community group that didn't represent extreme or deep religious convictions we found the Unitarian Universalist Church. Phyllis and I joined. These congregants were a marvelous, friendly group. I can relate one story that demonstrates how friendly. One of the women asked Phyllis if she could spend a night with me, just one night. My wife said no. Though we were members of that church for seven years I was never able to find out who that woman was.

When mother was visiting us, we drove her to a Friday night service. Another car pulled in alongside as I parked.

I said, "Mother, I'll introduce you to the driver of that car. He and I have the same name."

She asked, "Is his name Shelby Brandt?"

I said, "Yes!"

"Guess what?" she replied. "You were named after him. He was the baby I visited in the hospital while pregnant with you. I liked his name."

This was a good example of Synchronicity.

Our next encounter with organized religion occurred in a friend's basement. It was 1963 and a group of like-minded people was meeting with Rabbi Sherwin Wine. Sherwin founded a humanistic movement in Judaism that teaches there is no reason to believe in God, but that the Jewish religion's highest ethical traditions and the value of each person are what should be revered.

Yes, Sherwin was more than controversial. Members of the religious community vilified him. Newspapers identified him as Detroit's atheistic

Rabbi. He was denounced at public meetings. In the face of all the uproar surrounding Sherwin we admired him. He was a marvelous human being and the most gifted lecturer in the world. One evening Sherwin complimented me. He asked if I'd like to become a rabbi and help lead his movement. I was awed and grateful for his confidence but had to decline the invitation. My career was moving in another direction. In 1969 this splinter group became the Society for Humanistic Judaism. Their local house of worship is the Birmingham Temple in Farmington Hills, Michigan.

WHAT ELSE BUT AUTOMOTIVE?

Over the years a large proportion of my work was related to the automotive industry. I was either involved in productions of others or the development of my own productions. I'd always been removed from the business end of the auto industry. It was only many years later that I learned much of what had been going on regarding fundamental auto industry decisions. For example, at one point I produced videos for Volkswagen of America. At that time management of General Motors had been replaced by bean counters. These men no longer concentrated on either the development of better performing vehicles or vehicles providing longer lifetime ownership. Instead, they'd been concentrating on efforts to reduce manufacturing costs and increase profits. This left an opening for "the bug!" The smaller, economical VW.

Detroit treated the VW with contempt. In 1950 some 350 VWs were sold in the U.S. By the late 1960s U.S. Volkswagen sales averaged about 33,000 annually. The beetle became a success because it was everything it was said to be. A work of very sound engineering. Arthur Railton, Automotive Editor for Popular Mechanics said, "the VW sells because it is, more than anything else, an honest car. It doesn't pretend to be anything it is not." To compete, GM developed the Corvair. It was 1956 and GM recognized they had to offer something competitive to protect the low end of the market. Their answer was the Corvair. Some automotive people thought it had a chance to be a superb small car. But because it was a small car and not likely to make a large profit for GM, it was filled with compromises. Early tests reflected serious problems with handling. On sharp corners the car had a tendency to flip at high speeds. All of this was prelude to my involvement with VW in the '80s as producer and director of videos for dealerships. The attention my work received reflected VW's success.

While raising a family of four children I rarely took a vacation. Annual Auto Shows in Chicago and New York were always an important source of my freelance income. I'd also work the Detroit Auto show, as well as my scheduled TV or radio shift.

As an Auto Show narrator, I'd stand on a turntable extolling the virtues of the company's cars and trucks. Yes, I had the distinction of introducing the greatest automotive lemon of all time, the Ford Edsel, at the Detroit Auto Show in 1958. The wrong car at the wrong time. It died an early death.

On the turntable for Mercury. One of many Auto Shows for me.

One evening in Chicago a group of us Auto Show folks visited a nightclub. I'd always considered myself a fairly sophisticated city slicker, but when I saw guests of this club performing the latest dance I was shocked! It was called "The Twist." I never thought I'd see a public display as sexually oriented and revealing. I'd have expected the shaking of the derriere in that fashion would have taken place in a tent filled with Persian rugs, candlelight, and pot-smoking celebrants. This was a dance inspired by the rock and roll music of Hank Ballard and Chubby Checker. So much for bringing this television announcer into the 20th century.

On Jan. 16, 1967, Chicago's McCormick Place experienced a disastrous fire. It had been a magnificent location and was the venue for that city's annual auto show. Because of the fire we were informed this year our show would return to its previous home, the International Amphitheater, adjacent to the Union Stockyards. And housing would be at the Stock Yard Inn! What a switch! Chicago guidebooks noted, "Not to see the Stockyards is to miss seeing the real Chicago!" Carl Sandburg affectionately called it "Hog Butcher for the World!" Others sometimes referred to it as Sights, Sounds, Smells and Sex! Even Frank Sinatra mentioned the yards in his song "My Kind of Town." Now our neighbors would be farm hands, real cowboys, and other hard-working stiffs. These men weren't Hollywood extras. Among them would be rodeo riders of horses, steers, and wild bulls! This year at the Auto Show would definitely be different. Imagine! Beautiful models wearing gorgeous gowns walking through the legendary halls of the Stock Yard Inn.

WHAT ELSE BUT AUTOMOTIVE?

It was here that I was seduced. The Inn has long since been demolished, but the memory lingers on. She and I had been working together for a long time. This evening she talked me into taking her to my room. Who knows? Perhaps I was an easy touch. On the way we encountered a man who appeared to be so drunk he almost knocked us down. I later learned he was a private eye hired by her husband to follow his wife. The next day while we were on the turntable at the show her husband appeared. I was introduced to him. We shook hands and I immediately sensed a problem. This guy knew!

In short order the following occurred. George Hackett, consulting head of Ford's Display and Exhibits Department, asked me if I had a relationship with her. Gentleman that I was I of course answered, "Never!" For some reason the lady's husband was really disturbed. Not only had he complained to our boss, Mr. Hackett, but also after I'd returned home he called Phyllis. She listened to his story and gave me the phone. He told me to never see his wife again. My reply? Never! Not in this life! Not a chance! He threatened me and I ended the conversation by reminding him she had not been coerced. I said, "Remember the old adage? It takes two to tango." At this point some marriages would have collapsed ... ours did not!

In 1967 at the New York Coliseum, Ford Motor Company was introducing the new Mercury Cougar. The display included two live cougars behind a glass-enclosed area on the stage. That exhibit drew large crowds. At one point, however, activities took place that demonstrated our cougars were male and female. Curtains were drawn

Explaining the virtues of the new Mercury Cougar. The live cats probably on break.

and at an appropriate time reopened. George Hackett was an executive with a keen sense of humor. At the end of each show he'd always write a newsletter. Everyone working the program would receive a copy. In reference to what had taken place George wrote if any cubs resulted from that encounter, he'd make them available. As soon as I returned home. I placed ads in the London Times and in a newspaper in Tel Aviv with this simple copy, "Cougar Cubs." I then added Hackett's name and address. Several days after the ads appeared George telephoned. "Shelby," he asked, "Do you know anything about this?"

He'd received a call from a reporter in London. George told the reporter there were no more cubs available. We had a great laugh!

Forty-five years later in 2012 I received an email from an individual researching the Mercury Cougar. He'd found the above Cougar Cubs story. Loved it. Looked up my address and wrote how much he'd enjoyed it. Proof anything appearing on the internet is there for posterity.

How did Christa Kindt come into our lives? A stroke of luck I'll attribute to my automotive work and the Chrysler Corporation. If this were a novel, the events that brought Christa and her family to America would have appeared like a chapter written to move the story forward.

Bavaria, 1946. Six-year-old Christa, younger brother Klaus, mother Ruth and father Herbert.

At 17 Christa began a three-year apprenticeship in the German film industry. Her teacher and mentor was a 72-year-old assistant film editor. Christa's 6-foot height explains why they were called "Brains and Legs."

Erna Greif, Christa's wonderful teacher.

WHAT ELSE BUT AUTOMOTIVE?

Klaus, Christa's younger brother, played a significant role in what happened next. He was studying engineering. A victim of the flu, Klaus was at home reading the German edition of the Reader's Digest in which Bill Lear of Lear Jet had written the article, "How to Become a Millionaire Today." The Reader's Digest was the bible of middle-class America. Klaus wrote a letter to Lear saying he'd like to work for him in his California plant. He liked his ideas. The year was 1962. Lear answered saying he didn't have a job for him in California but would sponsor Klaus, and invited him to work in his Wichita, Kansas plant.

Soon Klaus was living in Mrs. Barnes' rooming house. For $13.50 a week she packed a lunch, washed and ironed a clean white shirt each day, and sent him to Mr. Oglesby's used car lot. Klaus bought a car for $350. Several months later Oglesby called and said, "Klaus, bring that car back! I have a better one for you. No more money!" Klaus must have been a likeable guy. Oglesby's dealership is still in business.

A year later Lear told Klaus that someday he'd be a very good engineer. Lear knew talent when he saw it. Klaus retired several years ago as a vice president of the Sony Corporation. When Lear told Klaus he could use another worker as industrious as he, Klaus revealed his father had two engineering degrees. Lear said, "Let's bring him over!"

Christa didn't want to leave Munich. She had two things. A good job as a film editor and a boyfriend. Her mother pleaded with her to give America a chance. Remember, she said, her trade, motion pictures, was a major industry in the United States. So, she honored her mother's wishes and came to Kansas. Surprise! The only job for an editor in Wichita was to work for the newspaper. No one even knew what a film editor did. So, like the rest of the family, Christa went to work for the remarkably talented and innovative Bill Lear.

At this time, he was developing the eight-track radio and cartridge to be used in automobiles. He hired Christa to work in the laboratory testing this new device. Since Detroit was the center of the automotive universe Lear bought a plant in the motor city. He sent Christa as the first employee to operate the testing lab.

Klaus in Mrs. Barnes' rooming house.

Excited to be working at Lear!

Klaus and father. Always time for a little shop talk.

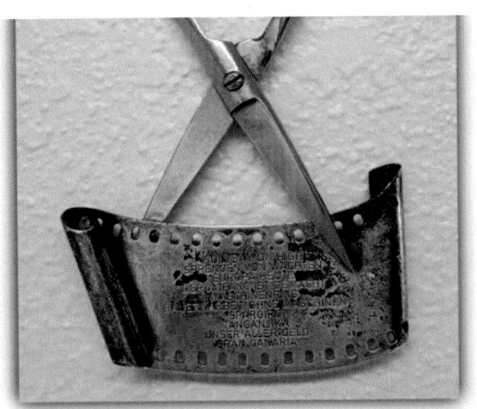

Christa's first editing scissors. A bon voyage gift from a friend.

Titles of award-winning films she edited are engraved on the 35mm film.

WHAT ELSE BUT AUTOMOTIVE?

Passing the time on her way to America. Christa pulls Bingo numbers with the ship's recreation director.

Working again. But not the way she expected.

It was at this point that Ruth, her mother, learned something few people know even today. The film industry was a major force in that town, Detroit. The precursor of all business and industrial communications in our country was Jamison Handy. Incidentally, Jamison earned two Gold Medals swimming in the Olympics. He operated two motion picture studios in Detroit. Union production crews as professional as those in Hollywood manned these facilities. During World War II the Jam Handy Organization had produced over 7,000 training films for the military. Detroit was called "The arsenal of democracy!" All manner of military equipment from tanks to trucks to military arms were produced in great number. My mother worked as an aircraft inspector in a Detroit plant. German Air Marshall Goering was reported as having said, "The Americans only know how to make razor blades." Four years later with the Luftwaffe in tatters, Goering said he knew that the war was lost when American P-51 Mustangs appeared over Berlin escorting waves of bombers. The record of American war production is staggering and in large measure determined the outcome of the war.

Before leaving the subject of Jam Handy I must make reference to one of the films in which I appeared that was produced by the Handy Organization. In 1955 the national Church of God headquartered in Anderson, Indiana commissioned Handy to produce an historical film about their church. "Heaven to Earth" was a story of the Church of God Reformation Movement. This was part of its Diamond Jubilee commemorating 75 years of fellowship, service, and witness. At the age of 29 I was cast as the founder of the church. We have a DVD copy of that film. I confess I've always wondered if I was chosen for that role because I may have been the only Screen Actors Guild member in Detroit who neither smoked nor drank.

By 1966, in addition to Jam Handy's studios, there were many other production companies in town. Christa's mother Ruth also discovered what a major firm Handy had become. Among their national corporate clients were Coca-Cola and Lucky Strike cigarettes. Ruth immediately traveled to Detroit to see if she could find film editing work for her daughter, Christa. Her experience was discouraging. She was unable to make contact with any of the production companies in the city. Ruth couldn't get past the secretaries.

What happened next is yet another example of a stroke of luck! A man whom I knew, Ken Williams, head of the Chrysler Corporation in-house film unit called Christa's home. He'd heard a rumor that there was a film editor on the loose in town and he needed one. At last! Christa was back in the film business. Her first assignment required editing and finishing three films and 10 slide programs. She knew what to do. Christa contacted a talent agency, auditioned narrators, found one both she and Ken thought could do the job and booked a studio for the recording session.

WHAT ELSE BUT AUTOMOTIVE?

Many automotive scripts can be just beautiful descriptions of an automobile. Others can be very technical. Fortunately for me she chose one of those more demanding technical scripts for the first recording. The session began and Christa discovered the narrator with the great voice could read well but was unable to pronounce many of the technical terms. He had to be dismissed. It was wonderful! Now she was desperate. Her first job in America and she'd chosen a narrator who couldn't do the job! Christa turned to the recording engineer for help. Where could she find a good professional narrator at this late date?

A scriptwriter couldn't have set up the next sequence better than life itself. I was on duty at the NBC television affiliate in Detroit when the call came for me. Jim Hartsel, one of United Sound's studio engineers was calling.

United Sound Systems Recording Studios at 5840 Second Avenue in Detroit's New Center area should be a museum as Detroit's first major recording studio. It opened in 1933. Jim Syracuse and his wife Esther owned the old house. Their son Joe was the recording engineer. Over the years many talented artists passed through its doors. It's the location where John Lee Hooker recorded his first song, "Boogie Chillen'," in 1948. In 1959, Berry Gordy Jr. recorded the first Motown Records song. Others who recorded here include Jackie Wilson, Marvin Gaye, Aretha Franklin, Parliament Funkadelic, Red Hot Chili Peppers, Stevie Wonder, and the Rolling Stones.

All of us in radio and television did freelance work at Detroit's recording and film studios, so let's make this clear. Jim could have telephoned any one of dozens of our town's narrators, each of whom could have done the job. But my extraordinary good luck was at work. He called me. First, Jim described this producer's predicament and the amount of work that needed to be done. It was substantial, at least two days of work. You can imagine my reaction. I immediately got a replacement for my shift at WWJ-TV downtown and quickly drove to the United Sound studios. I made sure to leave my white horse outside.

Yes! I can tell you what Christa was wearing when I entered the room. What an impact! This lady was definitely European. Not dressed like our American women. Very beautiful and in trouble. What a wonderful opportunity! I took off my suit coat, undid my tie and in two days recorded all 13 scripts. But, even more important, I realized this marvelous, beautiful, talented woman was a film editor and I'd been dreaming of leaving the talent end of the business to become a full-time filmmaker. I couldn't have written a better script.

Christa has since edited every film I've made! These productions have earned four EMMYS, three Cine Golden Eagles, the Landers Award, two gold medals, many blue ribbons including one from the New York International

Film Festival, and many other honors. I'd never before been teamed with someone as talented and intelligent as this beautiful gift from Europe. It was and remains an amazing experience.

Just a footnote about luck and my association with United Sound Systems Studios. In 1960 an older member of the Detroit News stations announcing staff, Pierre Paulin, and I began a school for announcers. We used the United Sound studios as our classrooms. Soon the Paulin-Newhouse School of Announcing was in business. The undertaking was successful! Each of our classes had as many as 30 students. Occasionally Pierre and I did have some differences. After two years I sold my share of this enterprise to Jim Garrett, a WJR announcer.

A full classroom at The Paulin - Newhouse School of Radio and Television Announcing.

WHAT ELSE BUT AUTOMOTIVE?

On Sept. 15, 1964, while visiting my father-in-law's cottage in Wild Fowl Bay, a Detroit News reporter tracked me down and called. The earth-shaking news? The day before, on September 14, Pierre had been shot and killed. I was incredulous! Apparently, the school had become a den of iniquity. Pierre, a well-known upright leading Catholic layman had become a heavy drinker. Evening sex parties were taking place at the school. A student's husband arrived and demanded to know where his wife was. Pierre, drunk and seated at the studio's console turned lights on. Through the glass the man's wife could be seen clearly engaged with a male companion. The enraged husband shot and killed Pierre, then ran into the studio and killed both his wife and her companion. Yes, I was stunned! Unbelievable! What a tragedy. My departure from that business and our association had clearly been a timely and correct move. Yes, an incredible stroke of luck!

MEADOW BROOK HALL

Working in television was a great training ground for producing, directing, and writing. Case in point, my film, "Meadow Brook Hall," an early chapter in my filmmaking history. It all began one evening after a meeting of the Board of Directors of Friends of Oakland University. I was in attendance as a member of that board. Woody Varner, the university's chancellor asked me to stay and chat. He wanted to talk about Matilda Wilson, the widow of automaker John Dodge. Would I be willing to tape-record an interview with this 82-year-old benefactor of the university? Mrs. Wilson's Tudor mansion, Meadow Brook Hall, was considered one of the 15 finest homes in America. It is now the fourth largest historic house museum in our country and is identified as a "National Historic Landmark." The Chancellor asked that I tape her recollections of the building of her home and the acquisition of its treasures if Mrs. Wilson would agree to a recorded interview. These treasures included a Rembrandt painting and many other wonderful works of art. I asked, "Why a tape recording when we could make a film?" He replied, "Photographers had never before been granted access to the mansion and its museum quality art." The prospect of walking through the home of the legendary Mrs. Wilson as she shared her personal history and the story of the building of Meadow Brook Hall was a once-in-a-lifetime opportunity.

The Chancellor and I met with Mrs. Wilson, one of the wealthiest women in America, honorary Lieutenant Governor of Michigan, first woman to sit on the board of a major bank, philanthropist, and businesswoman. Time magazine cited her as the "most prominent woman in U.S. Banking." She accepted our proposal to film and my feet never touched the beautiful parquet floor as we left. Talk of a stroke of luck.

Since I was employed by the Detroit News owned television station, WWJ-TV, I suggested they might be willing to provide a crew and equipment. I presented this proposal to Ed Wheeler, Vice President of the Evening News Association and General Manager of their stations. He was very receptive to the idea of the film and pledged cooperation. Since Ed had given the project the green light the television station's Program Director had to fall in line. But Shelby Newhouse had gone over his head, had not moved through the chain of command, and besides, the Program Director only knew me as a staff announcer. Who was I to take on such a project?

Mrs. Wilson was informed the Detroit News was undertaking the film as a gift in honor of her many good works. Months passed; my superior continued to manufacture excuses for not starting the film. Determined to go ahead, I asked Jim Jewell, a cameraman with whom I often worked, to volunteer his talents and equipment. Christa contributed as editor, United Sound Systems let us use their equipment and facility, only charging for the sound engineer and recording stock. I directed, wrote the script, and performed the narration. Costs absorbed by the university were only $3,000.

Why had Matilda selected Oakland County farmland for the building of Meadow Brook Hall? The answer lay in the location of her brother-in-law Horace's estate. That mansion was in Grosse Pointe, Michigan. Matilda and Anna, her sister-in-law, were less than friends. Indeed, they despised each other. Anna Dodge believed Matilda came from a working-class family and represented a social group far beneath her. Before his death, John, Matilda's husband, had been developing a Grosse Pointe property that included a man-made promenade reaching out into Lake St. Clair for docking Horace's yachts. But Matilda, after being snubbed by Grosse Pointe society, abandoned John's Grosse Pointe dream. From 1926 to 1929 she constructed the $4 million Meadow Brook Hall.

Horace and John were the Dodge brothers of the automotive empire bearing their name. In 1921 they were attending the National Auto Show in New York when John was said to have contracted pneumonia. Horace had him taken to their private railroad car. They returned to Detroit where John died. Newspapers of the day protected the reputations of the wealthy and powerful. Today, the more salacious the details the faster they are revealed and brought to the public's attention. The world of the '20s was told John Dodge died of pneumonia. However, while researching material for my films I was able to use the Detroit News morgue (library). I found a handwritten reporter's note in the John Dodge file. It contained a word we rarely see or use today. It said John Dodge died after a night of debauchery in New York. With the death of her husband Matilda inherited $75 million.

The widow Dodge joined her church choir. Lumber broker, Alfred G. Wilson and his fiancée sang in that choir. That relationship soured as Wilson's and the widow Dodge's flowered. Extensive newspaper accounts of the Dodge/Wilson wedding, June 29, 1925, made no mention of the jilted former girlfriend. However, a reporter's handwritten notes referenced interviews with choir members and others that revealed a deep sense of betrayal.

The following year Mrs. Wilson commissioned the Detroit architectural firm of Smith, Hinchman & Grylls to design and build their 110 rooms Tudor revival style home. Matilda went to Europe accompanied by a young member of the architectural firm. They spent months traveling about England and the continent studying residences of royal families and their friends. It was reported she would enter a manor house, walk into a room, and simply say,

"This one." And the room, down to the smallest detail, would be duplicated at Meadow Brook Hall. For a period of many years after I began work on this film visitors could simply press a button on the wall and hear a recording of my voice. They'd learn about the room's construction and its original location in Europe.

Though Matilda Wilson didn't attend high school, she did go to secretarial school. Her interest in young people and education was serious. She arranged the gift of 1,400 acres of her Rochester, Michigan farm for the building of a college campus. Then added an endowment of $2 million, tax-free. Oakland University began as an adjunct to Michigan State University. My daughter, Erin, was in the second graduating class. Soon that tie to the older university was dissolved. Today Oakland University stands on its own. Meadow Brook Hall and the farm's remaining 126 acres were bequeathed to the school when Matilda died.

Research in preparation for Mrs. Wilson's on-camera interview and our filmed walk-through of Meadow Brook Hall revealed more of a dysfunctional Dodge family history with its share of tragedy. Wealth could not save the life of a daughter who died of measles in childhood. The loss of her son, Danny, was another terrible blow. That chapter could have been written as a screenplay. The family had property and a home on Manitou Island in Canada. It was there that 21-year-old Danny met and fell in love with a tugboat captain's daughter, Lorraine McDonald. Danny then defied Matilda's pleas and wishes and they were married.

Manitoulin was the playground for many of the rich and famous. Danny owned a luxurious lodge overlooking the North Shore. The young couple spent their honeymoon at Danny's estate. He discovered a box of dynamite in the garage and lit one of the sticks. It exploded. Lorraine, the caretaker of the property, and the caretaker's wife rushed out to investigate. Danny lit a second stick just as the trio arrived. He attempted to toss that stick out one of the open windows. It hit the frame setting off a huge explosion. All were injured but Danny suffered the most. He lay unconscious on the floor, thought to be bleeding to death. To save Danny's life they carried him to his mahogany resort speedboat, the MAC, attempting to reach the hospital in the small town of Little Current. But this was one of the stormiest days of that summer. As they headed into four-foot waves Danny Dodge and the caretaker and his wife were in the back. On their journey around the island Danny regained consciousness. Lorraine heard Mrs. Bryant scream and when she turned around and looked Danny was going over the side of the boat. He apparently stood up only to be washed overboard in the rough water of Honora Bay. Newspapers across the nation carried the story. Once the body was recovered one paper quoted doctors as saying Danny Dodge's injuries were so severe, he could not have survived. His mother was devastated.

Did Danny fall from the boat, was he pushed out or thrown overboard? These were questions never to be answered. Could this have been an attempt to gain his wealth and estate through murder? There was speculation that Danny's death 13 days into his marriage was the result of an infamous plot. The family was so prominent that even though this occurred in Canadian waters the Detroit Police Department dispatched three detectives to assist in the investigation. Death by drowning was the ultimate verdict. No foul play could be proven.

The new bride sought compensation. There was a trial. Lorraine was awarded the luxurious lodge and a large inheritance. Murder or accident? It still remains a mystery. These tragic events occurred in 1938. Had the year been 1968 or even more recent, a Hollywood producer would undoubtedly have produced a major multi-million-dollar spectacular based on the drowning of Danny Dodge.

A documentary filmmaker looks for moments of truth, the unfolding of the unexpected, when something obviously unplanned occurs. One such moment arose during the filming of our project. It was delicious. While seated across from Mrs. Wilson I asked how she and John Dodge met. There was a pause, a smile, then . . . the answer. "Why . . . I was his secretary." I had to leave that in the film.

The final day's shooting was from a small two-seated helicopter. I will always retain the image of the cameraman and me using the same safety belt. I also held on to Jim's pants belt as he leaned out of the open bubble to shoot aerials of the estate and Matilda standing on the terrace below. She loved Percheron horses. Two days later Matilda was in Belgium buying these horses when she had a stroke and died. This truly amazing lady was full of curiosity and boundless energy. At 82 she still visited her office in Detroit's Fisher Building three times a week. When she and her secretary drove to Iowa to attend a series of events Matilda would do the driving. Both the housekeeper and her husband were available during the day to attend to her wishes. But each evening they'd return to their home and Matilda Wilson would be alone in that huge Tudor manor. Alone with art valued at millions of dollars.

With the death of Matilda my original script had to be scrapped. Everything we'd filmed would now be viewed in a new perspective and with added significance. For archival purposes alone Chancellor Woody Varner's foresight in requesting a recording of Matilda Wilson's own views and recollections now assumed increased importance. The film had its premiere on the campus of Oakland University in the University Theater. My mother, Rachel, was visiting us at the time and had the pleasure of being present.

On reflection, the opportunity to spend time with Matilda, this great lady, and enjoy unprecedented access to every nook and cranny of her home was a fantastic experience. At 82 years of age she was filled with energy. Actually tired me out. I would also characterize her as being down to earth. Mrs. Wilson spoke of having been raised on a farm in Ontario. More recent research suggests her parents had a bar in downtown Detroit. On occasion I just can't repress my sense of humor. Can't resist telling listeners Mrs. Wilson died two days after I shot her.

I offer the following as a footnote. Mrs. Wilson's attorney, Nelson L. Meredith, was the executor of her estate. He and her secretary conducted an inventory of the contents of Meadow Brook Hall. This inventory took a year to complete. Estate taxes were paid with monies raised through the sale of art such as the Rembrandt painting and other extraordinary treasures. The loss of these works of art further increased the value of our film for archival purposes since it became the only record of the home as actually lived in by the Wilson family.

INEQUALITY AND EQUAL JUSTICE

I performed as talent on all types of radio and television programs, doing thousands of newscasts and interviews in studios and at remote locations, and working as freelance talent all over the country. The direction in which we were moving as a nation was troubling. For those of us aware of serious issues affecting the very heart of our country it was necessary to respond to the most fundamental of our problems. Problems affecting every citizen. That issue was inequality. The unfulfilled promise of equal justice for every citizen. The right to enjoy all those freedoms granted to us by our constitution.

It was 1955 in Montgomery, Alabama. Rosa Parks, frightened but tired after working all day, refused an order from the bus driver to move to another seat so a white passenger could sit down in the section reserved for white folks. Despite the 1954 Supreme Court civil rights ruling in Brown v. Board of Education, a decision that reshaped America, black men in Montgomery could still not protect their wives. Black women were powerless to protect their children. Police were called to the bus. Rosa was taken to jail, fingerprinted, and charged with violating the city's segregation laws. This led to the boycott of buses by blacks.

A young 26-year-old minister named Martin Luther King Jr. rose to prominence during this episode. His oratory thrilled the crowd.

> If we are wrong, the Constitution of the United States is wrong. If we are wrong, God Almighty is wrong. If we are wrong, Jesus of Nazareth was merely a utopian dreamer and never came down to earth! If we are wrong, justice is a lie. And we are determined here in Montgomery to work and fight until justice runs down like water and righteousness like a mighty stream.

Black citizens of the city prevailed. The attendant national publicity moved me yet another step closer to my dream of producing an educational film about the contributions of Black Americans to the growth and development of our country. A film I hoped would be screened in every high school in our country.

It all began in 1960, when I was serving on the Better Human Relations Sub-Committee of the Michigan Department of Education, Curriculum Planning Committee. Now that's a mouthful! Try saying it aloud. Service on this prestigious committee was the result of yet another stroke of luck. Phyllis' dad, Herbert McCreedy.

Herb was a true member of an Irish family with his love of life and sense of humor. Yes, there was a certain amount of drinking. And one of Herb's favorite sayings was this toast. An Irish friendship wish:

May there always be work for your hands to do,
May your purse always hold a coin or two,
May the sun always shine on your windowpane,
May a rainbow be certain to follow each rain,

May the hand of a friend always be near you; your heart be filled with gladness to cheer you: And may you be in heaven a half hour before the devil knows you're dead.

But for me, what defined him most was his political activism. He was deeply involved in affairs of the day, advancing many significant contributions to public education, race relations, and labor. Community colleges and Junior colleges benefited greatly because of his efforts. One of his most important achievements was leading the battle to bring about the one man, one vote concept in Michigan. When I was a young man, we used to say the cows outstate were voting, thereby putting city dwellers at a distinct disadvantage. A city dweller's vote had less influence on the make-up of the state legislature than did a rural inhabitant's. Land, not population was used to determine the outcome of voting. Herbert McCreedy and Gus Scholle led the successful battle for one man, one vote. When he retired in 1967, he was serving on many national Boards and was head of the CIO, (Congress of Industrial Organizations) in Michigan.

Though the extent of my formal education had only been high school I served on many statewide committees. Whenever a state committee would request inclusion of a labor representative, Herb would often ask if I'd like to join that committee. These requests really represented another educational opportunity. The civil rights movement was in full swing. I whole-heartedly agreed with that movement's objectives and also served on both the Birmingham-Bloomfield Better Human Relations Committee and the Michigan Anti-Defamation League. I even participated in undercover missions for the ADL, attending meetings of organizations like the John Birch Society and returning with reports of their activities and publications. Often their views went beyond politics. They reflected antisemitic sentiments. It was evident they never viewed me as being Jewish.

While serving on the Department of Education Curriculum Planning Committee I learned that school textbooks did not include any of the history of African American contributions to the growth and development of our country. I was told it would take decades before school textbooks could be changed to include that history. I knew I didn't have to wait. Here was a need, an opportunity! Yes. I would make a film.

After 18 months of research and writing that included a visit to Harlem's Schaumberg Library and a meeting with University of Chicago historian Dr. John Hope Franklin, I had a script. Dr. Broadus Butler of Wayne State University approved my work. Both Dr. Franklin and Dr. Butler were African American. Broadus had even served as a member of the famous World War II Tuskegee Airmen. His contributions and encouragement were major factors in my final product. Perhaps most important was his assuming the responsibility of verifying the accuracy of our content. A single error would have invalidated, poisoned the authenticity of the entire project. But all of this was prelude, the easy part.

Though I'd produced educational materials for Encyclopedia Britannica Films several years earlier as Newhouse Productions, Inc., I didn't offer this project to them for several reasons. Perhaps most important was my desire to have my film reach the largest possible audience. I chose not to burden the price of each print with the kind of distribution costs Britannica would demand. Remember, I was determined that this film be placed in the library of every high school in the country. Each print's selling price would have to be as low as possible.

So now I was faced with every independent film producer's basic problem. Production funds! Where would I get the money? The hunt was on. I spent the next seven years visiting civil rights groups, religious organizations, petitioning foundations and government offices searching for funds. All to no avail. While I continued my frustrating search the intensity of the civil rights movement was growing. By 1969 many poorly produced, and historically inaccurate materials were being brought to a burgeoning market. It was now or never.

Britannica Films educational film catalogue included over a thousand titles. Not a single one of these was about African American history. It was time to visit Britannica. I was convinced we needed each other. For me, this was to be no ordinary presentation. I refused to leave the script for their review. Instead, I insisted on my reading it for those committee members present. Upon completion of the reading, they thanked me and immediately offered $16,000 in exchange for 50% of the project. Though my script couldn't be produced for $16,000 I was elated and forged ahead. Dug a hole for myself by adding $15,000 I didn't have. Every penny of the $31,000 went into production. There were no fees for producing, writing, directing, editing or narration.

It may be interesting to see how producers employ psychology to overcome possible objections to scenes they want to use. One of the darkest chapters in our history concerns the lynching and burning of black men and women. How would I get a picture of a lynching past my conservative

Britannica partners? I searched for the most graphic, offensive picture available. I found one that would move you to tears. Its message was clear. Men, women, and children were shown smiling and looking up approvingly at the strange fruit hanging above them. This is what I screened at the approval stage knowing it would not be accepted. But it gave me the opportunity to assure Britannica's representatives that this particular shot would be replaced with a more artistic and acceptable image of a lynching.

The Department of Defense owns a vast library of motion picture footage stored at the National Archives in Washington. J. Hoberman, university professor and film critic for the Village Voice noted, "If the Pentagon wants to go into the business of leasing to the movies (footage it owns) it should be open to whomever wants to lease and can afford to." In 1969 permission to use any of this material was controlled by the Pentagon's film office. It had the power to say yes or no to any request whether it came from Warner Brothers' major studio or Shelby Newhouse.

In my research, I discovered scenes critical to the success of the production of "Heritage in Black." Donald Baruch, head of the film office, said no; we couldn't have all the scenes on my list. He insisted we could buy similar footage from commercial sources such as stock footage libraries. I argued our limited educational film budget made that impossible. Besides, I didn't want something similar. I wanted the precise scenes I'd requested. He stood by his decision.

A careful study of Defense Department regulations suggested a possible basis for approval. Permission would be granted if use of the requested material would accrue to the best interests of the United States. This was the decade of the '60s, the civil rights movement, a time of civil unrest. I returned to the DOD citing this as my rationale. I pleaded that this production would definitely accrue to the best interests of the country. I argued civil strife arising from racial animosity and ignorance of contributions of Black Americans to the growth and development of the United States posed a serious national problem. The answer remained "no!"

It was time for another stroke of luck. My brother-in-law, Ward McCreedy, held a low-level position in President Johnson's administration. I called Ward. We discussed my project and the problem I'd encountered. The next morning a letter appeared on Baruch's desk from Paul Nitze, Deputy Secretary of Defense, and former Secretary of the Navy. It referenced the dispute. Nitze demanded action on the issue. Up or down, immediate action. Imagine the consternation in Baruch's office. Who is this Newhouse? How much clout does he have? Baruch knew a way had to be found to settle this issue before it got out of control. The footage in question wasn't worth jeopardizing his relationship with the undersecretary. We negotiated. I got all the footage I wanted. Everything! But his terms were tough. I had to agree to the screening of my film at the Pentagon before it could be released.

This was Baruch's turf. I could just see his friends, employees, and associates in the screening room supporting him and being critical of the film no matter what I produced. I knew I needed an audience with no ties to the Department of Defense. I turned to HEW, the Department of Health, Education and Welfare. After explaining my predicament, I invited these educators to the same screening. They were eager to participate. Now the Pentagon would have their supporters and I'd have mine. Encyclopedia Britannica Films, our production's distributor, would also send their Government Relations representative to the event. We finished the editing. All postproduction was completed, and I returned to the Pentagon.

The screening room was packed. After my brief introduction the lights were dimmed and the signal given to roll the film. An intense and lively discussion followed the screening. As anticipated, audience members associated with the DOD engaged in attempts to disparage elements of the film. Even an African American employee of Baruch had a negative response. The educators loved it. Our rebuttal, endorsed by HEW supporters, carried the day. There was no reason to prevent its release.

Just one year later, in 1970, the Department of Defense developed an 18-hour race relations course. I was told it was mandated that every serviceman and servicewoman in the military be required to attend. The curriculum included two films. One was a CBS production. I was overjoyed to learn the other was my "Heritage in Black." Translation? Millions got to see the film.

I insisted that as many African Americans as possible be employed in this production. Though I myself had been recording voice-over roles for decades I engaged the services of an African American NBC announcer for "Heritage in Black." I believed he was a far better announcer than I. We recorded the track in New York. Afterwards I walked the streets of Manhattan for hours, unhappy with his reading. Yes, he was a better announcer, but he couldn't touch my work as a narrator. This required a difference in style. He just didn't have it. Late in the afternoon using a street payphone I called the studio and asked if they'd stay open long enough for my return and another recording session. The answer was yes. Tired as I was, I went back and read the script. It's my track on the film. One passage, of which I remain very proud, that still moves me today, that will forever embody the essence of my film's message is the following:

> Through state laws, through violence, many citizens were denied their right to vote, denied equal education, denied housing, denied employment, denied justice. Yet the black man kept faith in the promise

of America. These are his words "We do not believe that things will always continue the same. The time must come when the Declaration of Independence will be felt in the heart, as well as uttered from the mouth, and when the rights of all shall be properly acknowledged and appreciated. God hasten that time. This is our home. Beneath its sod lie the bones of our fathers; for it, some of them fought, bled, and died. Here we were born, and here we will die. This is our country."

Dana, my composer son, has scored all of my productions with the exception of "Heritage in Black." For this film I went to Detroit's Motown group and hired an African American composer/arranger.

"Heritage in Black" had its premier before a distinguished audience in Detroit. It was held in the Detroit News auditorium. Present were members of the federal judiciary, politicians, educators, representatives of civil rights organizations and church groups. That week I was also invited to visit Dillard University, a private, black liberal arts college in New Orleans, Louisiana for the southern premier of our film.

A prominent figure always presented an address at the annual dinner of the national meeting of the NAACP in New York. That year instead of a speech, the honored position was reserved for a motion picture, "Heritage in Black." What seems an innocuous film today prompted questions in 1970 like, "Won't young black men riot after seeing this?" Of course, young men didn't need a film to open their eyes. They knew the conditions revealed on the screen. They lived them.

The honors kept coming. Over 3,000 educational films were produced that year. Instructional Media Directors in school districts across America purchase films for their schools. They voted to identify the 25 most distinguished productions of the year. "Heritage in Black" was among those winning this prestigious Landers award.

In my view perhaps my greatest honor came in 1963 while work on the film was still in process. I was asked to deliver the commencement address at my alma mater, Detroit's Cass Technical High School. This was 19 years after my graduation. By this time the student body was about 20% African American. Here was an opportunity to take advantage of the research I had done for my script. I spoke of the many outstanding contributions to our country made by African American citizens. In my address I commented on the wonderful opportunity these Cass students had been granted to develop relationships with those of other races. They were about to leave the protected environment of the school and enter the real world where they'd find many who would look down on these relationships. These individuals would attempt to perpetuate racist attitudes of past generations. I said don't let them get away with it. Help them understand these are your friends.

Premier of "Heritage in Black," in the Detroit News Auditorium. Daughter Erin, editor Christa Kindt and husband.

Greeting Dr. Miller at the "Heritage in Black" premiere.

A segment in the film, "Heritage in Black" touched on African American participation in the segregated United States military. However, it did not address the long delay between the order to desegregate and compliance. I knew President Harry Truman signed Executive Order 9981 on July 26, 1948, ending segregation in all branches of the armed forces. Yet two years later in 1950, the all African American 24th Infantry was deployed in Korea. Ninety-eight percent of the Army's African American soldiers still served in segregated units in April 1951, almost three years after Truman issued his Order. Later, during the United Nations Action in Korea the military finally complied.

Were they compelled to desegregate or was it voluntarily? My research had never revealed the answer to this question. However, the puzzle was solved in a most unlikely location: the cafeteria of The Detroit News, Michigan's largest newspaper.

General S.L.A. Marshall, a font of knowledge and marvelous raconteur was the paper's military analyst. I had access to the cafeteria as an announcer at WWJ, the radio station owned by the publisher. Sam and I would meet for breakfast. His storytelling abilities made it difficult to return to work. Two of his books, "Pork Chop Hill" and "The River and the Gauntlet" had been made into successful motion pictures. These were stories of the Korean War.

The General was familiar with "Heritage in Black" and knew of my interest in African American history. One morning we talked of segregation in the armed forces. I asked if he could explain the Army's delay in compliance with President Truman's Order and what finally prompted integration?

"Delay," said Sam, "could be explained by the strong opposition to integration at the highest levels of command. Much of the Army clung to old sentiments and practices for the same old reasons. The result of prejudice common throughout American society."

As an army historian assigned to the Korean conflict General Marshall had been charged with deploying trained interviewers to question soldiers immediately after action in combat. These were men fighting at platoon and squad levels. Sam told a story my research for "Heritage in Black" had not uncovered.

His field study with troops immediately after battle revealed a simple, but compelling fact. When American forces were routed and driven back to the Pusan perimeter in the south with positions overrun and many units disorganized, those soldiers integrated by chance, thrown together midst the chaos of combat, had put up the greatest resistance. These units had shown themselves to be among the most effective fighting groups in the battle.

He cited specific Korean actions. Among them: November 1950, when Company B of the 9th Infantry Regiment U.S. 2nd Infantry Division was temporarily led by an African American officer. They were fighting on the

Chongchon River Line. Sam wrote an article for The News in 1956 describing that company as possibly the bravest unit in that action.

Armed with the results of his study, Sam flew to General Douglas MacArthur's headquarters in Tokyo. He reported his findings and vigorously defended their message. It may be argued MacArthur lacked political judgement, but as a superb strategist with victory as his principle objective integration became a foregone conclusion. I had the answer to my question. Having seen military efficacy demonstrated in the heat of battle Army leaders finally accepted integration. General S.L.A. (Slam) Marshall played his role in moving us toward a more just, more democratic, more effective military.

In October 2011, while cleaning out old records, I came across my file of materials for the film, "Heritage in Black." There were many photographs and documents resulting from my research for that production. Discarding these made no sense. Christa and I immediately arrived at the same conclusion. The entire file should be donated to the Charles H. Wright Museum of African American History in Detroit. The appreciative museum staff accepted the collection. They were particularly pleased to see that each picture and document included the citation identifying its place of origin.

BEHIND THE CAMERA

    Though still on staff at WWJ, I devoted every spare moment to a new venture. I formed the Shana Corporation in 1968 to produce, direct, and write motion pictures and videotapes.

    One of my most interesting clients was a company called Caterair International. They provided in-flight meals for airline passengers in many different parts of the world. My crews and I loved it because it required shooting both in the United States and overseas. We worked on airplanes, at airports and in many foreign cities. Always flying first class.

While filming in France my schedule made it possible for us to have a free day. I could do anything I wished. This was my very first trip to Paris so my client, an African American named Bill Murray, and I chose not to play the role of tourists. We didn't visit a single guidebook location. Turned up our nose at one of the most famous streets and one of the most expensive strips of real estate in the world. The Champs-Elysees! Instead we walked through the streets and neighborhoods where average Parisians live, work and play. We did this for seven hours. It was wonderful. For us this was Paris. What stories to take home! Among the many sights and scenes was an entire carcass hanging outside a butcher shop. Talk about advertising! It was the first time I'd ever seen anything like that!

The real Paris, 1993. With Bill Murray and cinematographer Pat Lobzun.

And guess what? We had to finish every film in eight languages! English, French, German, Spanish, Italian, Portuguese, Russian and Swedish! For us, Caterair International was a money-making machine. A stroke of luck!

Caterair videotape releases. Ready to ship worldwide. From left: Martin Hogan, Christa Kindt, and Andy Thompson.

There were failures along the way as well. They tend to keep you humble. For me . . . my nemeses have been sports. Football players in particular. Not the men in the trenches, but real stars! A film titled "To Rescue Our Young from the Sexual Revolution" called for interviews with role models from the world of sports. I scheduled an interview with a National Football League player, an all-time great, one of the best backs in the game and a truly modest individual . . . soft spoken, very religious, devout . . . with an impeccable personal reputation. The film was completed and just as it was about to be released a story moved over the news wires; made papers from coast to coast; was carried on radio, TV, and cable. Our star had fathered a child out of wedlock. Hardly a model for this film. This very decent man acknowledged he was the father, accepted his responsibilities, and made arrangements to care for the child. His appearance in our film had to be cut before it could be released.

Then there was that NFL quarterback. Again, I was working on a film directed at boys and girls. The message? Safety! How important it is to wear a helmet while riding a bike. Everyone agreed. This quarterback would be a great person to carry the message. I traveled to his hometown . . . filmed him, his kids, their classmates at school . . . and went home happy as a clam. One week later the New York Times carried his picture on the front page. The story? His son had called 911. The boy's father had his mother on the floor and was choking her. My frustrated client cancelled the project. Well, you can't win 'em all.

Producers get assignments in a variety of ways. The most typical is being asked to bid on an RFP, a Request for Proposal. I received an unusual RFP. The client wanted to produce a film that would be used as an orientation piece for jurors in courts. Two years had been spent in research and the writing of a script. We would often get a set of specifications, but it was unusual to be given a complete script. The RFP letter indicated nine production houses were being solicited. I was familiar with all of them. Three were in Michigan, two in California, four in New York. Wilding and The Bill Sandy Company, previously the Jam Handy Organization, were the other Michigan firms. Both were major production companies with their own studios, large staffs, and their own equipment. Inclusion of my one-man corporation on that bidding list must have amused them. I felt the odds against my getting the job were even higher when I discovered the principal researcher and writer of the script was a vice president of the Sandy organization. And if that weren't enough, he and the client, a Wayne State University professor, were close personal friends.

Since the original grant had been generated two years had passed, during which time researching and writing of the script had been completed. I analyzed, studied the script, and prepared a budget. Then I did something unprecedented. Explained what I believed was wrong with the script. I argued it was a didactic teaching tool that would be used with a captive audience, a jury, and put them to sleep. All too often training films do exactly that. Act as a soporific. And guess what? There's minimal communication with a sleeping viewer. I wrote what I thought was needed was a screenplay. In my response, I included a treatment, describing my approach, what it would cost and a sample scene.

Winning that contract was most satisfying. Satisfying to me, mystifying to the competition. In this case being bold paid off. My script went through a lengthy and critical review process. The list of those reviewing this material was very impressive: there were federal and state court judges, U.S. attorneys, prosecuting attorneys, civil and criminal defense lawyers, law professors, and ACLU representatives. If the film were ever to be challenged in court by a losing party and found to have shown or stated anything resulting in a mistrial it could be very costly.

Because our cast included 48 principals (speaking parts) and 80 extras, the production process would be like shooting a mini feature film. Our budget wouldn't allow us to pay Screen Actors Guild rates. It was time for another stroke of luck. We met with the local Detroit SAG Board. Because of the public service nature of this film, they agreed to negotiate a special rate for the actors.

Casting was done through a cattle call. That means no individual meetings set up by agents. Come one, come all. Sit and wait your turn to be interviewed to read for a part. The most important role required an elderly woman. Any production can use some serendipity, and this was no exception. Unknown to us a very experienced performer was among the several hundred waiting to be interviewed. Mary Reynolds had a running part on a television series, "The Waltons." She was vacationing at her family home in Milford, Michigan and had read about the audition. Mary was growing tired of waiting and was about to leave when one of my assistants came to me and said I had to see this woman. She really looked the part. The moment Mary opened her mouth I knew we'd been blessed. Sixty-eight-year-old Mary was perfect. She was both a fine actress and a wonderful person.

While interviewing prospective actors my wife Phyllis was helping me with the paperwork. An incident occurred which I must note at this point. It involved a very beautiful girl, me, and a stapler. I was no novice. Had used staplers before. We've all used them. This gorgeous girl walked up to our table for the interview. I picked up the paperwork and promptly stapled my finger to the documents. Phyllis said nothing. The interviewee said nothing. I extracted my finger. No. This young lady did not appear in my film.

Our locations included the Michigan Federal District and Wayne County Courts. Bill Dear, my Director of Photography, had shot several of my previous films and had done an excellent job. Years later, after he'd become a director of feature films in Hollywood, Bill thanked me for the opportunity to shoot this film. It was a chance to test his skills doing a screenplay with actors and a large cast instead of the documentaries and industrial productions he'd been shooting.

One of many collaborations with Bill Dear. On the set of "Passport to the Past," at Greenfield village along with Phyllis McCreedy and Ray Troutman.

The client insisted that a real judge portray the role in our film. I was unable to dissuade him of that notion and soon I was in Washington, D.C. auditioning a federal judge. Think of that for a moment. How do you tell a federal judge he's auditioning and may not get the part? I couldn't bring myself to do it. We had a pleasant chat. I crossed my fingers and scheduled the shoot around his court calendar. He did a great job.

The completed juror orientation film was screened and carefully scrutinized by the same distinguished group that approved the shooting script. After passing this hurdle we ordered 100 prints for distribution. The cost exceeded $10,000. Then a federal judge who had not been among those who had seen the original script viewed one of the prints. She questioned language used to demonstrate the distinction between a civil and criminal case. This was a subtle point, but it could not be ignored. All the prints had to be destroyed. Our script had said, "In a criminal case a law has been broken." But this judge pointed out, "a law has not been broken until a jury so decides." A fine point perhaps, but the line had to be replaced by a new scene which we then shot and edited into the film. A second 100 prints were ordered. Filmmaking can be expensive!

The federal grant required an academic study to test the efficacy of the film. This study proved the work to be outstanding. Its effectiveness was in the 90-percentile range. "And Justice for All — the Jury" was selected by the United State Supreme Court and used without a successful challenge in all federal district courts as well as 350 state courts for 20 years. It appeared on television and won an Emmy.

There are two different types of television Emmy Awards. I've earned one national Emmy and three Michigan Emmys. To receive a Michigan Emmy my productions had to compete against the productions of other Michigan filmmakers. To qualify for a national award your program must have appeared in 50% or more of all national markets. That means you can only qualify if your program appears on NBC, CBS, ABC or PBS.

I received a phone call from a vice president of WTVS, the PBS station in Detroit. She explained the Corporation for Public Broadcasting had advanced $40,000 to their station for the production of an hourlong documentary. The subject was "A Continuing News Story." A year had gone by, and the project was not completed. CPB was now requesting their program. The station's personnel had gone through three scripts. Still no program! I was told WTVS only had $5,000 left. Would I help them? I asked to see the results of their research, screen the footage they'd accumulated, and study copies of the three scripts they'd written.

Their subject was the Chrysler Corporation bail out. The station's newsman on the project was a pro, Andrew Kokas. After studying their scripts, reviewing the interviews they had shot and screening their researched footage I accepted the challenge. I shot an additional interview, wrote a new opening and closing, produced an amalgamation of their three scripts, wrote transitions where necessary and most important of all, discovered what I believed to be a priceless piece of material. They were in possession of this but had not recognized its value. In my view, this information by itself merited airing of the program. They had taped interviews showing industrialists, academicians, and United States senators all voicing the same observation. In clear and direct quotations they were all saying, "There is no such thing as free enterprise in America." In one fashion or another every economic area was subsidized or supported. It was dynamite!

We also demonstrated that the bailout by the government wouldn't cost the United States Treasury a cent. Lee Iacocca, leading the fight for Chrysler, was sensational. He had a mind like a steel trap. I was asked if I wanted to interview him. I answered it wasn't necessary. We had access to footage of all his testimony before every congressional committee on the Hill. I asked permission of Chrysler's Public Relations Manager to shoot my newsman's commentary in their Chrysler Design Center. Normally this was off limits to anyone outside the Corporation. Permission was granted. Christa also came into the station one evening and cut a montage for me. I gave the new script to our reporter, Andy Kokas, and then directed and shot his commentary.

Iacocca loved the show. He requested a copy of "Chrysler: Once Upon a Time and Now." The station's management submitted it to the Corporation for Public Broadcasting, and it was entered in the national Emmy competition.

Christa and I traveled to New York to attend the dinner and festivities, never dreaming my program, one of 11 nominees in its category, had a chance against ten other network producers. That group included Dan Rather and Bill Moyers. I was probably the most surprised Producer-Director in the room when the name of my show was announced as the winner of the national Emmy.

At times life can be stranger than fiction. WTVS seeking our help had represented another stroke of luck. Then, when my Emmy arrived, I had to return it. Why? They had mailed me Dan Rather's (of CBS). It was for another program that had won an award. He had received my Emmy! Yes, I enjoyed the exchange.

The National Academy of television Arts and Sciences Monday...

NEW YORK -- The National Academy of television Arts and Sciences Monday awarded 46 News and Documentary Emmys for work appearing on the three commercial networks, PBS and by independent producers.

The winners were selected from a total of 187 nominations and the awards were presented at a dinner at a New York hotel.

* * *

The winners included: Outstanding Analysis of a Single Current Story -- PBS's "Chrysler: Once Upon a Time and Now," Andrew Kokas reporting . . .

Emmy Awards dinner in New York. We couldn't have been more surprised or happier! Outstanding Analysis of Single Current Story! PBS.

ORGANIZED CRIME

I continue to experience the unexpected entering our lives. What happened in this instance would only have been believed if written in a novel. Fiction! Not the real world. No producer wants to make a film that results in a lawsuit asking for $1.5 million and where the plaintiff is a member of organized crime. This scenario developed as a result of my being a member of the Michigan Council of Crime and Delinquency. In that capacity I saw literature advertising federal dollars for a public awareness campaign alerting everyone to the dangers of organized crime. The proposal required matching funds to shake loose $60,000 of federal monies. I had no way of knowing if any other filmmakers were aware of the advertisement, but it was sure worth pursuing.

I approached a number of organizations and finally generated the dollars for the matching funds. These monies would come from the Ford Motor Company Fund and two smaller foundations. John Bugas, head of the Ford Motor Company Security Department and a well-known former FBI agent must have participated in the decision to assist me. Ford had been losing trucks transporting parts worth hundreds of thousands of dollars. The hijackers may have been organized crime associates. I prepared an outline of my project. The elements were to be an hour-long documentary, four radio spots, six public service television announcements, a commercial that TV stations could use to announce the scheduled airing of the documentary, as well as 650,000 pieces of supportive handout literature. All I had to do now was convince appropriate state agencies this was a viable undertaking and I was the guy who could do it.

It was imperative law enforcement agencies be on board. The necessary research and execution would not be possible without their cooperation. The first step was to speak to Oakland County's Organized Crime Task Force. I managed to get on the agenda of their next scheduled meeting. Members of this group included County Prosecutor Thomas G. Plunkett, the State Police Intelligence Unit, the county sheriff, and several chiefs of police. After stating my objectives and how I planned to achieve them the questions came thick and fast. There was a lot of skepticism.

A captain from the State Police Intelligence unit asked if I was afraid of being targeted by members of organized crime. I asked how long he'd been engaged in this work. "Twenty years," he answered. "Well," I said, "you look pretty healthy to me." I reasoned if I were working with and for law enforcement agencies there'd be no problem. I knew members of organized crime families are businessmen. Business, that's the bottom line. To do anything to hurt me would generate heat. Heat is bad for business. I was also fairly visible due to my many years in radio and television. And organized crime members would know I was not just another entrepreneur on his own but was working for the State. I felt secure. Discipline within the ranks of organized crime is well known. I would only have to be concerned if some maverick got so upset he'd take it upon himself to act.

The county committee moved to forward my request for support to the next level. I passed out six copies of my proposal and left the meeting knowing at least one or possibly two of those documents would be on the desk of an organized crime family member that morning. Those who study organized crime say their tentacles reach everywhere. At some level, every agency of government has been compromised. Corruption is a fundamental problem. And in a perverse way that became a protective device for me. Since the enemy will know every move I make, I will not be permitted to go too far. They will find a way of thwarting inclusion of material which might seriously affect their operations. There'd be no need to physically reach out to me. The key is to never do business with them. Doing business is to establish a lifelong arrangement.

The statewide committee invited me to a meeting. Present were an Assistant U.S. Attorney; Colonel John Plants, director of the Michigan State Police; county prosecutors; several chiefs of police; and Vincent Piersante, formerly Chief of Detectives, Detroit Police Department, currently Chief of the Organized Crime Division of the Attorney General's Office. After satisfying this group I met with Frank Kelley, Michigan's Attorney General. A $135,000 sole source contract was approved completing the process and we were on our way. This is a lesson on how many hoops a producer may have to jump through to initiate a project! Many meetings over the course of the next year included approval sessions at various stages of the production. There were always questions challenging what we were proposing to do. Some questions could easily be interpreted as attempts to introduce roadblocks rather than expressing genuine legitimate concerns.

In 2016, as we watched the Democratic national convention, we heard President Barack Obama refer to our obligations to each other as "citizens." This reference jarred my memory. Took me back to one of the many meetings with my clients on the organized crime project. These meetings were to check on the progress of our work. On one occasion Colonel Plants interrogated me, yes, interrogated me. Appearing to test me to discover my true motive in pursuing this project. As if I might have an ulterior motive. Could it be I was really representing these criminals? Seeing to it that nothing seriously damaging to their operations would appear in our materials? The director of the Michigan State Police was an expert at this type of an exchange. More and more questions came, the pace became faster and faster until I shouted out my reason for this project! "I'm doing this because I am a citizen!" Piersante couldn't have been more pleased. That meeting wrapped up immediately.

Three people became principal conduits through which our work would flow: Vince Piersante, of the Michigan Attorney General's Office, Chester Sylvester, Senior officer, Detroit Police Department and Sgt. John Gambotto of the Organized Crime Unit, Detroit Police. Vince Piersante and Police Commissioner George Edwards had appeared before a U.S. Senate Committee investigating organized crime. They had introduced a chart similar to a major corporation's table of organization. It showed photographs, names, even nicknames of the Detroit mob, including the Don, captains, lower ranking members and associates. New York city's large population supported five organized crime families. Detroit had only one such family. As part of my research a meeting was arranged with a New York detective working organized crime. The address was on exclusive Park Avenue, a street of limousines and doormen. But inside was a simple, sparsely furnished set of rooms. The theatrical set designed and built for television's "NYPD Blue" was the cleaned-up version. New York wastes no money on city offices.

Yes, there are many stories in the Big Apple and this detective seemed to know them all. Or he had a lot of time for leisure reading and screening of films at the movies. Some of his stories were too graphic to recount here. A typical tale described the Harlem acquisition of the sports wire, a money-making machine of considerable proportions. As the story goes all sports wire betting was controlled by one of the five families. Franchises were parceled out to others. A group of African Americans in Harlem wanted their share. So they kidnapped a member of the family and held him hostage to pressure that family to do business with them. Organized crime caved in, the hostage was returned, and Harlem had its sports wire. The family had kept their word. However, every one of the kidnappers was murdered. Their heads were cut off.

"Your Silent Partner," the project's 54-minute principal film, centered on a discussion led by Vincent Piersante. He responded to questions from a military historian, corporate executive, law professor, and a college student. I filmed this scene at Marygrove College. We would give visual support to each subject by either shooting original material or by obtaining existing motion or still pictures and documents. I planned a four-hour uninterrupted discussion covered by five cameras. Lunch was served while talking and filming continued. Wireless microphones had just been introduced. We imported them and a soundman from New York. He joined a very experienced union crew. However, there was one unexpected interruption, which could have been disastrous. At one point during the filming, a heavy film light attached to the ceiling broke loose and fell. I've never heard of such an accident on a film set. I've been associated with this business for most of my life. That was the first and only light that ever fell on a set where I was working. Fortunately, that light missed everyone and was quickly replaced. Had someone with access to our set been paid to disrupt the filming? Even worse, was this an attempt on Piersante's life? Was this an intended Mafia hit? We'll never know.

One of the lessons I learned by working with police is that if you must employ actors who are not professionals use cops! They're great. I suppose it's because they are always acting. Sitting in a patrol car, just the two of them, they're relaxed among friends. The moment they exit that vehicle to confront a situation, even to give a ticket, they take on that aura of authority, the expression that says I'm here now, I can handle this.

The placing of illegal bets through bookies was one of many topics we covered. To tell that story we needed to shoot at a racetrack, but the Detroit Race Course was owned by Joe Zerilli, the Don himself. Asking permission to use that track was out of the question. It wasn't available. Now hear this! The Royal Canadian Mounted Police rode to the rescue. Arrangements were made to allow my crew to enter Canada with all of our equipment, but without the usual restrictive paperwork. The sequence was shot at the Windsor Raceway. However, one scene appearing in that sequence was shot on St. John Island in the Virgin Islands. My wife Phyllis and I were on vacation. The scene showing an associate of the mob making a call from a phone booth was shot there. On yet another occasion the Mounties again came to our rescue. A member of the mob controlled the laundry that supplied linens to Detroit's expensive restaurants. They had a lock on that business. We needed to film an important scene in that environment and were concerned. To use a Detroit location meant the mob might hassle us disrupting our work. Arrangements were made for us to shoot at the Inn on the Park in Toronto. That restaurant sequence is now in one of our television spots.

Subtlety is not one of the mob's strong points. They send very dramatic messages. I had an experience that wasn't exactly a horse's head on our bed, but the message got through. My editor, Christa Kindt (eventually to become Christa Newhouse . . . but that's another story) and I were in her studio editing the film. It was the witching hour, midnight! As we opened the rear door to leave for the night the lamp above the door illuminated our two cars. There were some small stones on the hood of my car. Not Christa's, just my car. Some of the stories I'd been told immediately came to mind. I thought of the Detroiter who made the mistake of striking a member of the family. When his body was found both hands had been cut off. At one time an informer disappeared. A dead pig whose throat had been cut was found at the rear door of the bar the informer frequented. I must admit I was probably a little apprehensive given the subject of our project. The hour was late. Nonetheless I tried to reach Vince

Piersante in Lansing, our state's capital. There was no answer. I was able to reach Detroit Police Department officer, Robert Bulloch. Bob came right over and using his handkerchief carefully removed the stones saying they'd probably not find fingerprints but would run a test. He then checked under both hoods, declared things were okay and we could start our cars. We called it a night.

The next day I had a talk with the chief of police in Birmingham, the suburb in which I lived. After learning about our project and the events of the previous night he ordered frequent police car passes by my house. Without question, I knew they could get to you if that was their plan. Nevertheless, I no longer parked my car in my garage. I now parked under the street lamp. When I locked the car, I placed a broken match between the hood and fender. If the match was not there in the morning, I wouldn't start the engine.

My son Dana played the college student in the film's discussion. He also composed and recorded the music for the documentary. Christa synchronized all the voices, music, and sound effects, edited the film and we were ready to fly to New York to mix the tracks. Christa and I boarded the plane, but we weren't alone. Detroit Police Sgt. John Gambotto was with us. He carried his sidearm. Yes. John was armed on the plane.

We had reached the most vulnerable stage in the production. For the first time all the elements of the documentary were in one place. The sound tracks and images as well as the actual film negatives were all in Christa's studio. They'd be there for ten days. Piersante instituted additional measures for security. Each hour, on the hour, Christa checked in with the lieutenant at the local precinct, a squad car drove by frequently, and when we left for the night, an armed guard was posted in the studio to be relieved in the morning. The assigned officer would come from different law enforcement agencies. As a result, he would not be known and recognized by local officers. That almost led to an armed confrontation.

One evening the plainclothes unit patrolling the area had not been properly briefed. Lights were on in the studio and through the plate glass window they could see an armed man with both a rifle and sidearm. Neither the security guard nor local officers were in uniform. It was a dangerous situation. Fortunately, cool heads prevailed and identifications were exchanged. I can imagine there were a few choice words for the precinct officer who'd failed in briefing the plainclothes unit.

Our documentary was completed, approved, and 65 prints were made. The 54-minute film was then screened for a select group of law enforcement officers and prosecutors. Some complained the content was too tough. There was sure to be a lawsuit. The prints were scrapped, changes made, and a date set for a private screening at the home of Governor William Milliken. I took a print to Lansing where we joined our governor and his guests to view the final product. After the screening there was an interesting, serious discussion. In the end approval was given for its release. Prints were sent to government agencies, police academies, libraries, high schools, and Michigan television stations.

Our film showed photographs of 26 members of this Mafia family. We identified them by name, nick names and when appropriate, listed their so-called legitimate businesses. A lawsuit was filed against Chief Piersante, spokesperson of my film. The suit sought damages of $1.5 million. It alleged production of the film was the culmination of Piersante's personal vendetta against the plaintiff and his family. He contended he'd been libeled. Claimed he was falsely accused of being a member of organized crime and characterized as a criminal.

A lawyer from the Attorney General's Office defended Piersanti. Once again, truth is stranger than fiction. This lawyer was the son of George Edwards, the Detroit Police Commissioner who had posted the organized crime chart referenced earlier. The plaintiff threatened to make me party to the suit if I didn't cut out every section of the documentary showing pictures of or making statements about the person who was suing. He demanded those scenes also be cut from the master and each of the release prints. The three foundations who provided matching funds for the project were also threatened with being made party to the suit. None of us capitulated. All of us held with the State.

A subpoena duces tecum was issued requiring all my records concerning the project be sent to the court and I was deposed on two occasions. I testified for almost five hours. The case moved up and down through the courts for seven years. Its conclusion had a Hollywood screenplay quality. A court date was set and as part of the discovery process each party had to identify witnesses they intended to call. Frank Kelley, Michigan's Attorney General was a very clever guy. He made it known he was prepared to call both the plaintiff's wife and his mistress. Wife and Mistress? That did it. They threw in the towel and the suit was withdrawn. Among the terms of the settlement the state agreed to refrain from publicly discussing the case. Research that lawsuit? Forget it! According to the records it never existed.

I'm very proud of a letter received from Vince Piersante, Chief of the Organized Crime Division of the Attorney General's Office thanking me for my work on "Your Silent Partner." I carry a copy of this in the event I ever have a confrontation with law enforcement. Friends call it "My get out of jail card."

STATE OF MICHIGAN
DEPARTMENT OF ATTORNEY GENERAL

STANLEY D. STEINBORN
Chief Assistant Attorney General

In Reply Refer To:
81-1171

FRANK J. KELLEY
ATTORNEY GENERAL
LANSING
48913

May 6, 1981

Shelby Z. Newhouse
The Shana Corporation
451 North Eton
Suite E-7
Birmingham, MI 48008

Dear Shelby:

At long last the Civil Suit of <u>Jack W. Tocco v Vincent W. Piersante</u> over the showing of Tocco's name, picture, and business in the organized crime educational film, "Your Silent Partner", is over.

On April 16, 1981, Jack W. Tocco dropped his libel and slander suit against me for participating in the Movie as the moderator.

Your decision in making the Film and your forthright response to questions regarding the how, why, and by whom the Film was put together was certainly a factor in causing the final resolution of this most lengthy law suit.

On behalf of myself and the State of Michigan I thank you for your time and effort, but most of all for your willingness to stand up and be counted in the continuing battle against organized crime.

Sincerely,

Vincent W. Piersante
Chief, Organized Crime Division

VWP:bjm

    The evening before the 2012 presidential election, Christa and I saw Oliver Stone's excellent film "JFK." What a stunning feature film. Almost a documentary. The outstanding performance by actor Kevin Costner delivering a fantastic courtroom summation is unforgettable. I am not a fan of conspiracy theories, but the recitation of multiple government documents being marked not available to the court and therefore the public, will forever mark the case of the assassination of President John Kennedy as incomplete. I am reminded of President Eisenhower's caution regarding the military-industrial complex. Remember, there were powerful financial interests invested in the continuation of the Vietnam War. The power of the ability of our government to control and suppession courtroom evidence under the guise of national security is ever present.

Though not of national significance, my own personal experience concerning my organized crime film "Your Silent Partner" is a case in point. Recall my story of the negotiation between the Michigan Attorney General and Mafia boss, Giacamo (Jack) Tocco concerning the withdrawing of Tocco's suit about my film. That agreement required all public records of "Your Silent Partner" be expunged even though my project's financing came in large part from a government grant through LEAA, the Law Enforcement Assistance Administration. Search if you will through court records, law libraries, even Google, the lawsuit doesn't exist, but the film does. In fact, I have in my possession a 16mm print of my 54-minute film. Retired Sgt. John Gambotto also has a print as does the Michigan Attorney General's Office.

IT'S ONLY POLITICS

The Detroit News Page Three
Thursday, October 31, 1974 — SECTION A

A film flop

$83,250 crime movie is loser

By ROBERT M. PAVICH
News Staff Writer

An ill-fated film, "Your Silent Partner," probably typifies the federal government's efforts against organized crime in Michigan.

It flopped.

The film now blushes unseen, beneath a growing blanket of dust, in a seldom-visited closet in the Oakland County's prosecutor's office.

"The film was terrible," said Prosecutor L. Brooks Patterson. "It was worthless.

"I had to walk out on it after 20 minutes — I couldn't stand it. What claptrap."

Produced by the prosecutor's office under a $83,250 federal grant, the hour long film was intended to educate the public "on the realities of organized crime." The main story line is that mob elements prey on legitimate businessmen through extortion and physical intimidation.

The viewer thus learns how "the syndicate" uses its vast wealth to corrupt police, politicians and other public figures.

Patterson's decision to walk out in the middle of the film must have been a difficult one. At the time, he was an assistant to then-Prosecutor Thomas G. Plunkett — the Cecil B. de Mille of "Your Silent Partner."

Plunkett had obtained production money for the film through the Office of Criminal Justice Programs in Lansing. That office, in turn, doles out chunks of taxpayers' money shoveled to the states by the Law Enforcement Assistance Administration (LEAA) in Washington.

"Your Silent Partner" was intended to be shown to schools, service groups, libraries and law enforcement agencies around the state.

"No one has ever asked to see the thing," Patterson said. "It's been sitting on our shelves for two years now with no takers. I guess they heard how bad it is."

Coleman Alexander Young was elected the mayor of Detroit in 1973. He was Detroit's first African American mayor and served five terms. Coleman had been a member of the famous Tuskegee Airmen in World War II. He had not only worked as a former union organizer, but rumor on the street was he'd also worked as a runner for the group controlling Detroit's Numbers Racket. Perhaps that explains one of his first acts as mayor. He disbanded the Detroit Police Department's Organized Crime Unit. These police officers were sent back to local precincts. Among them was our friend, Sgt. John Gambotto.

Politicians, they're wonderful! The county prosecutor, Tom Plunkett, who participated in our organized crime project had to campaign for a new term. Tom was a Democrat. His opposition was L. Brooks Patterson, a Republican and member of Tom's own prosecutors' team. Patterson jumped on the bandwagon by using our project as a campaign issue. He claimed our film and radio spots represented an outrageous use of local taxpayer funds. A total waste! And guess what? Patterson said, "The work was lousy! It was poorly produced and not worth watching!"

Typical of many letters received from police academies, universities offering degrees in law enforcement, and others who purchased our film would be a request for a second print since theirs had been played so many times it was worn out! This from Western Michigan University. Yes, I felt vindicated.

WESTERN MICHIGAN UNIVERSITY
AUDIOVISUAL CENTER   KALAMAZOO, MICHIGAN 49001

November 9, 1976

Mr. Shelby Newhouse
Shana Corporation
464 Townsend
Birmingham, Michigan 48009

Dear Mr. Newhouse,

We are interested in obtaining a new copy of the film "YOUR SILENT PARTNER" as our copy is worn out. We received our copy in 1972, August and has been used frequently.

Please let us know the purchase price of this film or advise us as to how we can obtain a copy.

Your prompt attention will be greatly appreciated.

Sincerley,

Bernice Bigelow
Bernice Bigelow, Head Film Library
Audiovisual Center

In April 1974, Melville Hoover Jr. of Youngstown, Ohio, a university student, submitted a thesis seeking a master's degree in science. The subject was, "An Evaluation of Michigan's documentary film, 'Your Silent Partner'." The following hypothesis was tested: viewing the film "Your Silent Partner" does not significantly change awareness of organized crime among the public. The summary of this 82-page study contains these statements: "The film 'Your Silent Partner' did significantly increase awareness of organized crime. This research has shown that a public education film on the topic can increase public awareness of organized crime."

Unprincipled people may be found everywhere. I am personally convinced their tentacles have on occasion reached into the highest office of the land. Yes, in all political parties. All of which leads me to Two-Gun Cohen and all of his shenanigans. What a character! He played a major role in the Chinese revolution. Sounds like fiction, but it's history.

Morris Cohen was born in 1887 and spent his youth in a London slum. The eldest son of Orthodox Jewish parents he became an incorrigible juvenile delinquent and around 1900 he was arrested and sent to reform school. At the age of 16 he was shipped off to western Canada. There he participated in every form of thievery one could imagine. Cheating at cards, leading a band of pick pockets lifting wallets and purses. And what an environment! Gambling, liquor, prostitution, opium-dealing and confidence games all flourished. Private armies and bandits were everywhere. Cohen quickly became a regular in those smoky gambling dens. Those days Chinese in Canada were despised. Outgoing gregarious Morris picked up bastardized Cantonese and through his many contacts developed a relationship with Chinese revolutionaries.

The press didn't know what to make of this Cockney Jew. They wrote that Mr. Cohen is in close touch with Chinese affairs here and knows the men of the orient probably better than any man in Edmonton or Western Canada. Morris gained the respect of his Chinese friends by coming to the defense of a man being attacked by an armed robber. This rabble-rouser was told that the Manchu's who controlled China were not interested in the welfare of the people, but only in maintaining their control. He listened to his Chinese friends and got the message. China was ripe for revolution and this con man Morris could see personal advantages. He pledged to devote his life to the service of Sun Yat-sen. He sailed to China in 1922 and though he never learned Chinese did become an aide to Sun Yat-sen and a general in the Chinese Army. Chiang Kai-shek unified the country in 1926. For an astonishing historical biography I recommend, "Two-Gun Cohen" by Daniel S. Levy.

Two notes for which I can vouch. After typing the previous paragraph, I searched google and discovered the following:

> Bieber Entertainment Enterprises has acquired the rights to award-winning playwright Lionel Goldstein's screenplay *The Chinese General*, marking the second project in the works about Morris Abraham Cohen (a.k.a. Two-Gun Cohen) the adventurous aide de camp to China's first

modern president Dr. Sun Yet Sun. Denis Bieber is producing the $45 million movie. . .

Now hear this and see why Morris Cohen's story has a place in my story. The largest and most prominent of all the works of art in our home is a 3-by-6 ft. painting. We found it in an antique shop rolled up like a manuscript, had it framed and hung in our Great Room. The painting's subject could have been anything from seascapes to landscapes to flowers to famous cities to people to whatever. But it is a painting of the last dowager empress of China. The cruel vicious Cixi, a principal in the story of the Chinese revolution. A major figure in the tale of Two-Gun Cohen. Before becoming China's ruler, she became the highest-ranking concubine by killing others, was said to have caused the death of her own son, and when she lay dying in 1908, she had the emperor poisoned. In the language of the Bronx I'd say, "Go figure!" This painting hangs in our home, but Cixi is not a member of our family. We admire the work as a piece of art.

But how do you interpret the meaning of the following unlikely triad? One: My reading the biography of Two-Gun Cohen. Two: The information concerning the making of a film on his life. Three: Our painting of the last dowager empress, Cohen's greatest adversary. Some would identify this sequence of events as an excellent example of "synchronicity." In conclusion consider this: as you move anywhere in our Great Room, Cixi continues to stare at you. It's eerie. Enough to send shivers up and down your spine.

Relaxing in the Great Room under the watchful eyes of our lucky find.

Not too eerie after you've lived with her awhile.

A LIGHTNING ROD FOR CONTROVERSY

In 1976 after 26 years of broadcasting I left radio and TV and never looked back. To demonstrate the variety of projects which came my way, let me travel from contact with some of the wealthiest families in the world to an artist who came out of an agrarian Mexican revolution, Diego Rivera.

In 1932 Henry Ford's son Edsel was president of the Detroit Arts Commission. He and Dr. W. R. Valentiner, Director of the Detroit Institute of Arts, chose to engage this Mexican artist to paint murals on the four walls of the Garden Court of the museum. In 1978 Ford Motor Company executives chose me to produce a documentary on the subject of these Diego Rivera frescos.

Detroit Institute of Art Garden Court with completed frescos.

What an assignment! Cameramen all over town held their breath desperately wanting the opportunity to film the work of this world-renowned artist. I had never directed Bob Handley whom everyone knew as Pooch. Bob was a member of the Cass Corridor artists. This was a near-downtown section of Detroit looked down upon by many as a haven for prostitutes, artists, and pot smoking characters. I'd seen examples of Handley's work as the Director of Photography on several projects. Pooch almost cried in his effort to pursue me to grant him this fantastic opportunity. I hired him and have never regretted that decision. In large measure, due to his photography, the film, "The Age of Steel: Diego Rivera" won a well-deserved Emmy. It now resides in 218 libraries worldwide.

Another stroke of luck. While Rivera was executing the frescoes in 1932, George Pierrot was in charge of public relations for the Art Institute. George was eager to be interviewed. We knew each other since I often appeared doing commercials on his Channel 4 television travel show.

One morning Christa joined me at the museum. We studied the frescoes. I told her how I intended to introduce the artwork and though she knew my approach would work, she had an interesting but more dangerous suggestion. Why not simply move the camera dolly all the way around the four walls of the Garden Court without stopping? I told Christa that would be great, but extraordinarily difficult to execute. What a challenge. We shot three takes. Each was over three minutes of uninterrupted filming. As light was falling differently on each of the four walls the assistant cameraman riding the dolly with Pooch was continually changing not only the focal length but the aperture. The last of the three takes worked and is seen in the film. Yes! That shot lasts three minutes.

Preparing for a 360-degree dolly shot. Director of Photography Robert (Pooch) Handley behind the camera discussing details with Assistant Cameraman.

Few people are aware that Henry Ford had an intense interest in photography. He sent photographers all over the world to film anything and everything. When his son Edsel paid for the Rivera frescoes, Henry saw to it that the execution of this work of art would be filmed. The completed footage was then stored in Dearborn at Michigan's Ford Rotunda. The Rotunda had been designed by Albert Khan for the 1933 Chicago World's Fair. This historic building was eventually moved to a site directly across from Ford's World Headquarters.

Nov. 9, 1962, a disastrous fire destroyed the building. Fortunately, the Rivera footage was saved and then given carte blanche to the National Archives in Washington, DC. Though the Archives received the footage as a gift, I had to pay for a copy of this precious material to be used in my documentary. What a stroke of luck! We'd now be able to incorporate actual film of this world-famous artist's execution of the murals. I celebrated by singing "Luck Be a Lady Tonight." I chose to produce the first half of our film in black and white since this original footage was shot with this type of film. The second half is in full color.

A portion of the fresco on the Garden Court's north wall. Manufacturing at the Ford Motor Company's River Rouge plant.

My research led me to one of Rivera's assistants, a 68-year-old artist, Ernst Halberstadt. Along with my crew and Linda Downs, the museum's Curator of Education, we visited him in his home in Buzzard's Bay, Massachusetts. I took with me a section of the historic footage. We projected that film through a window on the porch to a screen in his living room. As we played several scenes, we recorded Halberstadt's comments. I'd been careful not to reveal our intention of showing him pictures of himself taken 46 years earlier. Soon there he was preparing the plaster for Rivera to use in painting the frescoes. When that footage came on the screen there was a pause in his commentary, then an emotional response. His insightful observations were a great contribution to our film.

The next morning as we were preparing to leave his home Halberstadt excused himself and went into his studio. He returned carrying a huge glass bowl containing many small vials of paint. These were actual samples of the paint Rivera used on the murals. He suggested we take them back to Detroit as a gift to the museum's conservation department. Everyone immediately recognized the value of this contribution. Should there ever be a need to touch up a mural they would now have the actual color with which to match the original. What a gift!

When the frescoes were completed in the depression year of 1932, there was a huge outburst of criticism. Some thought it was an effort to depict Detroit and the automotive industry as unfeeling oppressors of these workingmen and women. A mixed chorus of praise and rage descended on the city. Critics demanded the murals be covered or destroyed. Among other concerns, attention was drawn to the vaccination panel. Some said it deliberately mocked the nativity of Jesus. However, Rabbi Leon Fram of Temple Beth El said the frescoes speak of the deepest religious lesson. "The lesson that man, plain common man, possesses the potentiality for brotherhood."

The Detroit News published Rivera's response to this chorus of criticism. He said,

> My Frescoes were inspired by a belief in the worker. I'm a worker myself. I know the worker. And I have painted him as I know him and see him. I understand the struggle of the worker. And I have tried to put in these frescoes that struggle, as I understand it. I painted these walls out of my heart. I could not have done the work if any restrictions had been placed on me. I'm an artist and this is my own work as an artist. If I painted what other people wanted me to paint then I could not regard myself an artist.

To protect Rivera's work auto union members had to stand guard at the museum. Detroit Institute of Art Director Dr. W. R. Valentiner and DIA Board

Chairman and donor Edsel Ford defended the murals in the press. They refused to permit modification, covering, or destruction.

Common sense prevailed and as Rivera himself said, "You come in two hundred years, these paintings will still be here." I included many of the artist's own words in the narration describing his message and mission in doing the work. Edsel Ford paid Rivera $10,000. Then, because of the 1932 economy, President Roosevelt closed the banks. The Ford Motor Company lost over $32 million, and Edsel had to pay the $10,000 a second time. These were some of the results of President Roosevelt's drastic action.

We had produced many scripts in Spanish and knew that the most easily understood, purest accent comes from Columbia. However, for the role of Rivera I knew I had to have an authentic Mexican accent. I traveled to New York and only auditioned Mexican actors. It was time for yet another stroke of luck. A distinguished actor and filmmaker, Carlos Montalban was available. He was absolutely perfect! Carlos was Ricardo Montalban's brother.

The musical score to any film will always play a significant role. But that score's importance is magnified when accompanying a project that has art as it's subject. Dana, my composer son, recognized the Diego Rivera film as a rare opportunity to provide a major contribution. His score was wonderful. In addition to a beautiful Latin theme, he composed a particularly descriptive movement for the section of the frescoes that depicts the pouring of boiling liquid steel into a huge industrial bucket. The work truly comes to life through his music.

We finished "The Age of Steel: Diego Rivera." I joined Linda Downs, Curator of Education and Dr. Frederic Cummings, Director of the museum to screen the film. Where would you expect to find the greatest freedom of expression? My guess would be in the world of art. Why then would a director of a major museum suppress a work of art? We may never know because Dr. Cummings is no longer with us. At the conclusion of the screening I was astonished to see Dr. Cummings was unhappy. More than unhappy. He was furious, incensed, apoplectic! I was baffled. I thought the film was great and calmly asked what had disturbed him? "What was the problem"? Fred came up with several innocuous rationales such as he didn't like the sound of Ernst Halberstadt's voice. As a filmmaker whenever I have the good fortune of having found an actual participant in the events being depicted, I'd choose that person over the best narrator in the world. There surely was more to this than Halberstadt's voice. Fred also disliked the accent of the actor playing Rivera. Remember . . . in my effort to be absolutely authentic I didn't just audition Spanish-speaking actors. I'd only auditioned Mexicans. Carlos Montalban as Rivera was perfect.

The Public Relations department of the Institute had planned and promoted a series of events to introduce our new film to the community. Despite Dr. Cummings' reaction to the work these arrangements could not be changed. Among the festivities was a screening and formal dinner for members of the Founders Society. There were other activities scheduled. The museum's theater would show our film every day for the remainder of the month. Cummings could not cancel all of this. But the moment things quieted down he suppressed the film. The director of a museum of art suppressing a work of art. Unthinkable!

It took some time to understand the Museum Director's problem with the film. I had previously produced an Henri Matisse film for the museum. He loved that production. It became clear that Fred had expected the same kind of treatment for Rivera's work. Fortunately, he'd never read my script. If he had this film wouldn't exist. I discovered Fred despised Mexican art. His doctorate was in European art. If it were possible, he'd have removed the murals from his museum's walls. He spoke disparagingly of art of the Americas. I believe he was actually ashamed of the frescoes. But above all, the most important objection was clearly political. I'm convinced Fred was afraid his wealthy Grosse Pointe supporters would be infuriated at Rivera's message and would reduce their contributions. In other words, Dr. Cummings was expressing precisely the critiques offered in 1932. His view was why spend precious time on the social history . . . the message . . . the politics of the art?

I believe my principal responsibility is to capture and communicate to my audience exactly what the artist is attempting to convey. I believe my film did just that and it was too much for Fred to bear. If you were an art teacher and wanted to show this film to your students, you'd encounter difficulty in acquiring it. But there was more to come. Several years later Fred got the brilliant idea of cutting a hole in the floor of the Garden Court to re-direct visitors to the galleries below. The immediate response of many in the community was to express concern that employing jackhammers would endanger the frescoes. This issue brought about a public reaction that was further heightened by an action taken by my Cass Corridor cameraman, Bob Handley (Pooch). Bob went to the Detroit Free Press and revealed the existence of our film, which was virtually unobtainable.

The uproar this news created was unbelievable. There were radio and television debates on the issue of free speech. Public meetings were called. Lawyers debated the issues at a public forum. They also argued as to whether a museum director had the right to suppress a work of art.

I remained above the fray. Fred could not. He called me in to negotiate. If I would agree to remove his and the museum's credits from the film, he agreed to give the film away to another institution. We had a deal. Christa removed the credits, and the film was given to the Walter P. Reuther Library, Archives of Labor and Urban Affairs, located on the campus of Wayne State University.

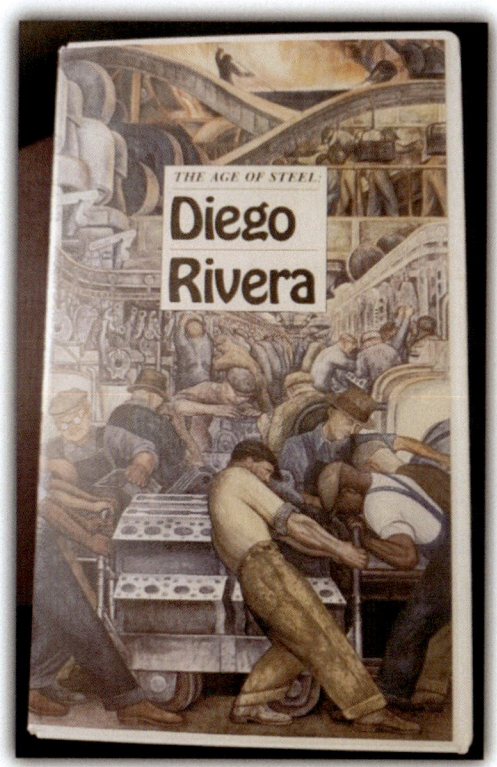

The Ford Motor Company Fund was my client. The following letter dated Aug. 16, 1978, came from Ray Kooi, Director of the Fund.

Dear Shelby:

Enclosed is a check in the amount of $4,166.66 payable to Shana Corporation. This is the final payment on our contract with you to produce the Diego Rivera Documentary film.

I want you to know how pleased I am with the results of your creative efforts. The film is first class, and more than meets our expectations. I know that you gave an extra measure to this project and want you to know that I realize it and appreciate it. The reaction of the viewers at last night's preview was very positive. I would say "mission fulfilled."

With regards,

Sincerely,

Ray Kooi

Some years ago, Christa and I were invited to visit a group on the campus of the University of Michigan at Ann Arbor. They were interested in both labor and art. I was asked to screen the Rivera film and answer questions. The young man who made the arrangements also scheduled an interview on National Public Radio. This NPR interview was set for a specific time. So, after showing the film and answering questions we left for the university studio and the NPR interview.

The girlfriend of the young man accompanying us ran up and asked, "Mr. Newhouse, did you ever live in New York?"

"Yes," I answered. "As a small boy I lived in the Bronx."

"Do you see that woman standing over there?" she asked. "That's my mother visiting me from New York. She was in your fourth-grade class, remembered your name and attended today's session. Her best friend was a girl named Shirley Margolis. Mother remembers something about a box of candy."

That incident in my life had occurred at least 50 years before. This was truly another example of synchronicity. But there wasn't enough time to talk with my former classmate. NPR was calling. Who says six degrees of separation? It's definitely only three.

EXPANDING HORIZONS

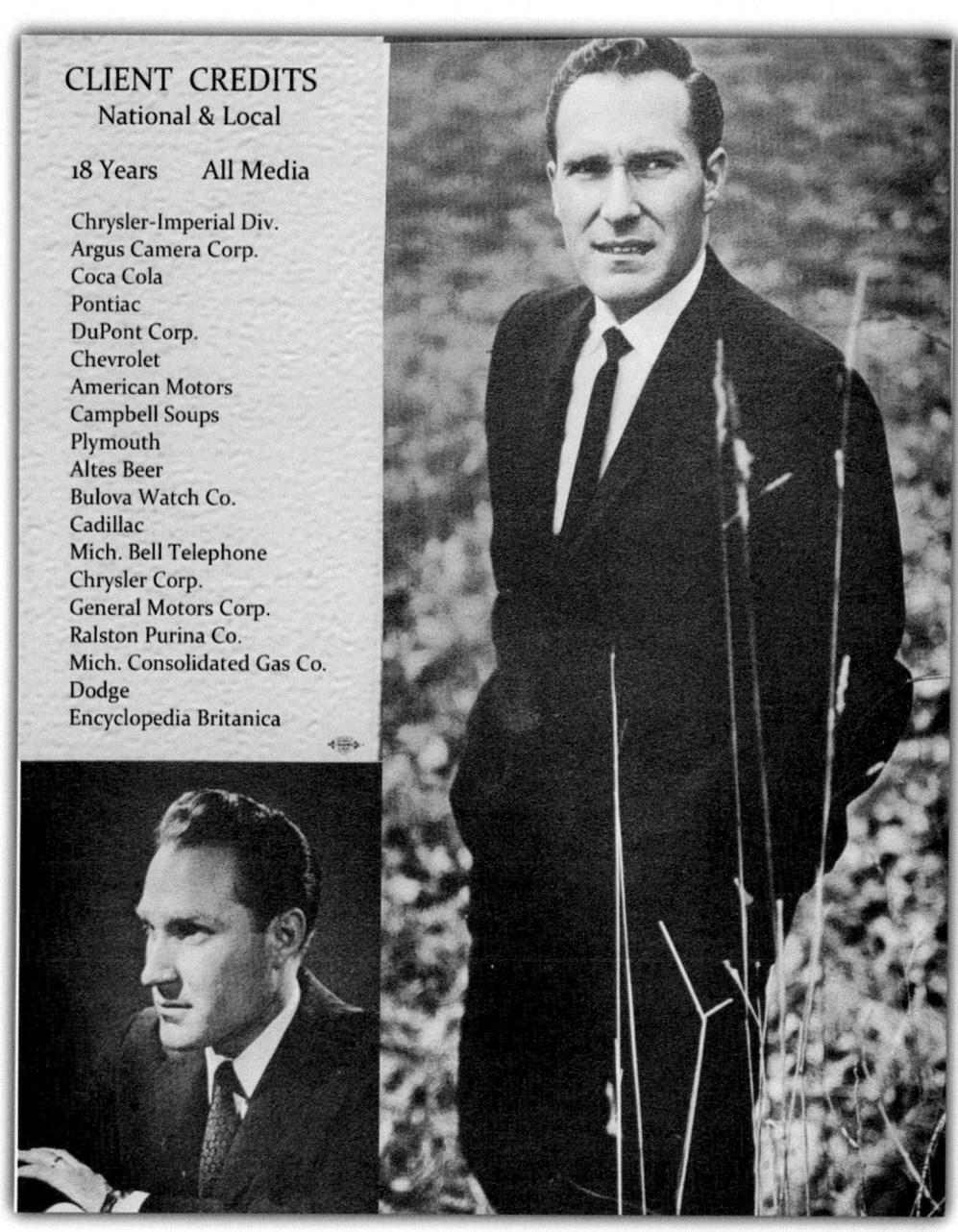

Seeking to advance my career I was always on the lookout for opportunities to both increase my earning power and associate with established successful organizations. There was a rumor going around town that Bob

Senglaub of General Motors was interviewing candidates for a Director/Producer position. I contacted his office, and an interview was arranged. Senglaub was the eccentric head of General Motors Photographic Department. As usual, having been a performer all of my life I arrived dressed as always, wearing suit, tie and winged tip shoes. I was ready to work before the camera. Not ready to work behind it. Senglaub was not impressed.

Not long afterward the national Oscar awards program was televised. Woody Allen won an Oscar. He didn't appear though he did send a message saying he was at home practicing his clarinet. Sir Laurence Olivier also won an Oscar. He appeared and gave a very eloquent acceptance speech. The very next evening the local Michigan Emmy Awards ceremony was televised. Winner's acceptance speeches were over the top. You'd think they'd achieved the most important wonderful award in the world. They thanked the sun, moon and stars as well as their most distant relatives. That night I was awarded an Emmy for my film, "Heritage in Black." For me, self-deprecation was the order of the day. It was just another stroke of luck. I thanked the powers that be and then said, "You know, I could be home practicing my clarinet. And by the way, in the event I won an Emmy I did prepare a statement. But it was purloined and read last night by Sir Laurence Olivier." That brought down the house. The next morning there was a call from Bob Senglaub. I spent the next two years working as a Director/Producer for GM Photographic.

My principal assignment was to Canadianize GM's American videos. GM of Canada, headquartered in Oshawa, Ontario, couldn't afford to produce their own videos. I would screen ours, list everything that denoted the U.S., and then research Canadian visuals to replace those I removed. Since Canada is a bilingual country, I also had to produce both a French and English sound track. This required many flights into Montreal and overnight stays at their hotels. It was wonderful! I vowed to visit every hotel in town and nearly did!

French Canada hated the English language. Whenever I got into a Montreal cab I'd say, "Bonjour Monsieur! Comment ça va?" The driver would respond with a mouthful of French, which I couldn't possibly understand. I'd interrupt him and explain I don't speak French but wanted him to know I respect his language. Montreal was fascinating. It was very European and because of the rift between the English and those of French heritage I did experience occasional negative encounters.

Years later, Christa and I were driving through the Gaspe Peninsula in Quebec with several of our dogs. We were looking for a place to spend the night. It was dark when I stopped at a motel restaurant and tavern to ask if they accepted dogs. The proprietors acted as if they didn't understand what I was saying, indicating they couldn't speak English. Finally, I began to bark like a dog. They responded to that universal sound. Their answer was yes! Yes, to

English barking dogs.

    Producing films and videos can be exciting and challenging. The need to travel adds to the complexity but also the enjoyment. Over the years I've had adventures shooting in the United States, Canada, France, England, Italy, Switzerland, Portugal, Chile, and St. John in the Virgin Islands. But have you ever traveled to a place that truly changed your life? We have. Bois Blanc Island!

    Geographically Bois Blanc is the lowest point of Michigan's Upper Peninsula. In 1884 the U.S. government opened Bois Blanc to settlers. According to the Cheboygan Democrat newspaper, 71 families settled there that first year. The U.S. Coast Guard opened a Life-Saving station at Walkers Point in 1891. That building is now used as a non-denominational chapel during the summer months of July and August. The Pines Hotel with 41 rooms opened July 9, 1888. The Episcopal Church of the Transfiguration was completed in 1905. Today, worshippers continue to attend services in its beautiful sanctuary. Pointe Aux Pins was the first resort community on the island. Prices to buy the cottages ranged from $200 to $500, and many are still in use.

    Much of Bois Blanc Island remains as the same pristine wilderness seen by early settlers. Fifty percent is State owned forestland containing White and Norway pines that tower 200 feet. The island provides habitat for Dwarf Lake Iris, Douglas Hawthorn, eagles, osprey, herring gulls and extensive and quite old beaver workings. By the early 1900s several sawmills were operating here. One mill, on the site of what became our island house, our Insel Haus, may have been the cause of the beautiful meadow surrounding our home. Workers at the mill were constructing wooden crates for commercial fishermen. We can readily assume they laid claim to the nearest trees. Today, we are the happy beneficiaries of their labor. The encroaching tree line began to recede leaving in its place our beautiful meadow.

    In 1958 Phillip Hart was elected Michigan's U.S. Senator. I produced his radio commercials in that campaign. Governor Soapy Williams asked me if I could help candidate Hart with his television appearances. After watching Phil perform, I told Michigan's Democratic party I was unable to help him. He was the perfect candidate. Absolutely natural on camera. So good I'd be embarrassed to suggest anything. While promoting the welfare of the common man and improving his quality-of-life Phil earned the name, "The conscience of the Senate." Some years later, in tribute, a U.S. Senate office building was named the Hart Building.

    Shortly before his death from cancer the senator's wife Jayne gave a party. I was in Washington doing research at the National Archives and made certain I'd attend. As she led Phil around the room, I took advantage of the opportunity to thank him for his service. I told him I felt as if I were speaking for all

Michiganders who couldn't be there that day.

Here's further evidence that life is often strange. As I write this, I'm sitting in my home on Bois Blanc Island in the Straits of Mackinac. Phil Hart was instrumental in getting federal funds for the building of our harbor and dock. He also played a significant role in bringing electricity to our island in 1967.

A submarine cable beneath the Straits of Mackinac carries electric power from the mainland to our island. Try living today without that source of power. That's really tough. Not often, but on occasion, storms or other natural phenomena as well as accidents interrupt our electricity. Most folks on Bois Blanc prepare for that contingency by having a gasoline-powered generator. I don't know of anyone else here who has a Detroit Diesel generator that puts out 20,000 watts! Our unit can provide enough electricity to handle 10 homes the size of Insel Haus. On one occasion our generator ran for 17 hours.

Senator Hart's connection to Bois Blanc Island stems from his marriage to industrialist Walter Briggs' daughter, Janey. She was incredible. An aviation pioneer and pilot who helped pave the way for women astronauts. She was among the first 10 women trained as astronauts. Janey also participated in the founding of the National Organization for Women in 1966. Her father was the founder of the Briggs Manufacturing Company. That firm played a significant role in the automobile industry.

Janey's sister, Susan, married a member of the Fisher family. We all remember the famous slogan, "Body by Fisher." A signature found on all General Motor's cars and trucks. The Fishers are among the largest landowners on Bois Blanc Island. They're benefactors of this incredibly beautiful limestone rock in the Straits of Mackinac. Senator Hart is buried 17 miles from here on Mackinac Island. Tragically, the Hart's lost one of their eight children on Bois Blanc. Their teenager drowned.

So what were the strokes of luck that brought us to Bois Blanc Island? In 1976 a bay window was being installed in Christa's Livonia, Michigan home. Her mother, Ruth, overheard a conversation between two brothers making the installation. They were talking about land their father owned on an island up North. This intrigued Ruth. She and Christa took her Olds 98 to Cheboygan, five miles across the water from Bois Blanc Island. They learned Captain Ray Plaunt could ferry them across the Straits of Mackinac to Bois Blanc. The 98 was huge. Like a real traveling living room! Its front bumpers literally touched the captain's rear end as he steered the boat. The 98's rear tires were on board, of course. But the large vehicle's trunk was actually out over the water.

It was October and the colors on the island were beautiful. They never did find the land of which the brothers spoke. Gene Babcock was the realtor showing them around. Like most men on the island Gene wore several hats. He was also a stonemason, master builder of fieldstone fireplaces and a dozen other trades. Later in the afternoon Christa was considering buying 80 acres in the center of Bois Blanc. "Yes," said Ruth, "it was beautiful, but it made little sense to buy land on an island and not be near water." They continued their search and saw the exterior of this house in which we now live, but it was not available. Not for sale. The living room fireplace had been built by the realtor, Gene Babcock. And there was a depression in the soil of the driveway. A dead crow was lying there. For Christa, a superstitious European, this was a sign of impending tragedy.

She spoke of returning to the mainland and home. Christa was scheduled to edit a film for a client. Me, Shelby Newhouse. Ruth insisted they couldn't come this far and not go over the five-mile-long famous Mackinac Bridge. Due to her childhood experiences in Germany during World War II Christa still has a residual response while crossing bridges. Our allies and we were very successful in bombing Germany's bridges. They kept rebuilding, we kept bombing! Nevertheless, mother and daughter rode across the bridge to the town of Hessel. A set of blue dishes in the window of an antique shop caught Ruth's eye. The shop was closed, and they couldn't find the owner. A sign in the window said, "Back in Ten Minutes." They asked the owner of the shop next door when the antique store would open. The answer? She went home for lunch. Walk a quarter of a mile this way, turn right at the big oak tree, then turn at the lilac bush and she'll be in the red house. Christa said they'd return at another time. "No," her mother said. "I'll never be back." Perhaps Ruth had a premonition. In a matter of months after their return to Livonia, she died on Easter Sunday April 10, 1977.

The depth of this loss was incalculable. Yes, it was the loss of a mother. It was also the loss of a business partner, for Christa had taught her mother to assist in the editing of films. There was also the loss of a grandmother who helped care for Christa's twins, Monica and Tania. Christa's father, the twins' grandfather, Herbert, in typical Prussian fashion, still expected his routine to continue. Dinner on the table as usual, menu the same as before, purchases of food the same.

35mm on the Moviola! Christa and her mother discuss a sequence.

Move ahead to 1980. Christa received a letter concerning land for sale on Bois Blanc Island. Gene Babcock, who had escorted Christa and Ruth on their tour of the island in 1976, had died. His family had given his notes to realtor Steve Begle and Steve contacted Christa. She decided to revisit the island and invited me to join her. I'd never been further north than Bay City and looked forward to the trip.

It was about a four-hour drive to Cheboygan and the ferry to the island. Steve met us. We discovered he had been raised in the house Christa had seen and admired on her first trip and it was now up for sale. Christa discovered she could buy it and 40 acres, or 184 acres. She loved the location. It included 1,800 feet of frontage on the Straits of Mackinac. The land continued over a mile to Lake Thompson, a beautiful inland lake that boasted its own island. Christa walked the beach picking up small stones and pieces of driftwood. They ended up in her pockets. Back home in the editing suite she couldn't keep from rubbing those rocks. The decision to purchase was in the stars. There was no way out. It had to be! And it was 184 acres . . . the whole cottin' pickin' thing! She bought everything, house and land, on Aug. 5, 1980. It was her 40th birthday.

Peter Fisher had owned the house. Yes. He was a member of the prominent family that manufactured bodies for General Motors cars. Peter was a very down to earth, friendly fellow known to all on Bois Blanc as Pete. He'd been using the house as the home base for his sailing, hunting, and fishing activities. A beautiful ship's wheel still hangs on the ceiling of the living room. This isn't a replica. It's an actual ship's wheel with a diameter of 5 1/2 feet. Eight electric lanterns are suspended from this lovely symbol of the sea. Pete had good taste. Tragically, Pete died at the early age of 42. He was alone in his sailboat participating in a race. A storm came up; Pete had a heart attack and died.

Christa began working on the old house almost immediately. Permits were obtained and building commenced. Her first decision was great. Christa hired a group of Mennonite carpenters from Indiana. They built kitchen cabinets, installed beautiful stained glass highlighted with fleur-de-lis designs. A local builder installed hardwood kitchen floors.

It was not easy to direct this project from a distance of 300 miles. In addition, I've learned building is very much like life. It isn't over until it's over. Christa forged ahead, though every trip north revealed errors made by these so-called builders. Indeed, there was a period of about three years during which time the house could be seen from Cheboygan five miles across the water. This occurred because its insulation had been applied but not yet covered. We called it the pink house.

A necessary consultation. Still a lot to be done and some unwelcome surprises.

Building inspectors? How important are these folks? When building on an island we've discovered they're very important. Our building inspector discovered a key beam holding up our roof was several inches short. What had the so-called builder done to overcome this obstacle? Nails had been used to bridge the gap. We hired and fired three builders. The last one actually went to jail. To acquire all necessary permits, we did hire an architect. He drew a plan that looked like the typical Northern Michigan motel. Fortunately, his drawings carried the notation "verify on location." Christa did a lot of verifying.

When Christa bought this home it had 3,000 square feet. Insel Haus now has 7,800 square feet. She designed the Great Room, nine bedrooms, two second floor studios, kitchens two and three, and nine bathrooms. There's even a marvelous suite in the basement complete with bath and shower. Christa turned a screened-in porch into the beautiful Veranda Room. She also built our attached 24-by-24-foot outdoor event room: the Gute Stube. (German for Good Room). All of the materials for this structure, even the large beams, come from the property.

Her sense of color and choice of furnishings created an environment that can best be captured by what a truck driver exclaimed upon entering the house. After looking around he took off his hat, tossed it on a couch and shouted, "Honey! I'm home!" The exterior of Insel Haus absolutely captures the island's character. It's an island home.

One day the building inspector made the observation that everything Christa had done concerning the design and construction of the home conformed to all existing requirements for a Bed and Breakfast. That idea hadn't occurred to us though we had planned for it to be a retreat center. We were living in a zoned community and Insel Haus was considered residential. It was important that we request a variance from the Township Board. It was granted, and Insel Haus became the first official Bed and Breakfast on the island. Christa and Steve Kruk, her graphic artist, designed a wonderful web site. We became permanent yearlong residents in 2001.

CHANGES ALL AROUND

In December of 1981, after 36 years of marriage, Phyllis and I agreed to end the formal, legal part of our relationship. There was a very amicable divorce. We discovered we'd have parted sooner but neither party wanted to hurt the other. Phyllis went to live with Veda, her widowed mother. They were drinking companions.

Many social changes had occurred during the '50s, '60s, and '70s in America. Phyllis had worked in the home raising our four children. They were now responsible, educated adults. Phyllis was an excellent model of the American wife and mother of our youth. Concentrating on the virtues of motherhood and home as defined in those years.

The following letter from Phyllis, written years later, is evidence a divorce need not lead to bitterness.

> Thanking you with deep appreciation for the role you played in fathering and raising our four marvelous children. I think they got the best qualities and talents of both of us. (As a mother I certainly wouldn't admit to any failures in my offspring.) Reminiscences are usually bittersweet; I look back with a mixture of happiness and sadness. I think of the good times with a chuckle and a laugh. The bad times are recalled with a tinge of tears. I wouldn't trade any of them away. Nor would I go back. Thanks for all your consideration since the divorce.
>
>   Happy Father's Day,
>   Phyl

The letter serves as further evidence of how lucky I've been. And of course, Phyllis' reference to consideration includes Christa. I feel compelled to add one more letter, also from a much later time, I believe completes the picture of our relationship.

> On Your Birthday   Jan. 15, 2005
>
> Dear Phyllis,
>
>   There I was a freshman in the Cass Tech auditorium hoping to land a role in the senior play. Then this beautiful girl sat next to me and started a conversation. How did she know I had never had a girlfriend? Not since Shirley Margolis in the fourth grade! And I was really uncomfortable speaking to girls. Reach into your memory bank. Phyllis, you were that

girl. We could not have known nor would we have believed the series of events that flowed from that conversation.

Our backgrounds were different, but clearly our needs were not. If scientists were able to harness the attraction it would have rivaled the most powerful magnet in the world. Among other things, I had none of the social graces and turned to you for instruction. My parents were loving and nurturing but caught up in a never ending need to stay afloat, to fight forces they couldn't possibly have understood during that time of the Great Depression. Herbert and Veda fought the same fight to feed and house you and Ward, but they engaged the world with intellectual tools and ideas as they tried to right the economic and social evils of the time. The New America organization was an example.

Through loving you I was given the opportunity to enter a new and different world. I reflect on this as I look back on our relationship and the central role you have played. One day as teenagers we walked along the street outside of Henry Ford Hospital and projected ourselves into the future. Remember? How many children would we have? Three, four, five? I count four as I sit here: Erin, Marc, Dana, and Kim. Your contribution to their character is beyond measure. In that most important basic fundamental part of their being they are good people. The lesson you taught by example was to have compassion for others. As we move through life we cannot escape hurting others, but let it be inadvertent, not by design. I believe we have transmitted that characteristic to the children. It may have been our most important contribution. Time passes, we grow, we change. What a roller coaster! You are now 80 and truly remarkable. You have survived the blows of outrageous fortune. Still beautiful, equipped with wit and humor.

Happy birthday from your once husband, always lover.

Shelby

Strokes of luck. Add the year 1982, another important milestone in my life. Christa Kindt was an educated European, working as a senior editor in the film industry. She was definitely not a product of the social forces defining the role of women in our American society. On Jan. 19, 1982, Christa and I were married. The location was the old Botsford Inn in Farmington, Michigan.

Photos of the wedding show us standing underneath a shotgun displayed on the wall behind us. Clearly, this instrument had no significance to our wedding. Our friend Rabbi Sherwin Wine performed the ceremony. Perhaps his most noteworthy comment was, "You're both old enough to know what you're doing."

Christa loved the wedding ring Phyllis had given me 36 years earlier. She asked me to keep it but make the same ring for her. Its message, written in Hebrew and translated by Sherwin reads, "She is more precious than the pearl."

We Do! Me, Christa, and Sherwin Wine (right).

A small reception with family and friends.

I did get more than I bargained for. Thirteen-year-old twins Tania and Monica and a menagerie of 12 cats and two dogs!

With Christa, Tania and Monica.

A STROKE OF LUCK

There was no time for a honeymoon. I had to leave for Hawaii the next day where I was scheduled to shoot a film for the Ford Motor Company. Christa had to stay to complete an editing assignment. The intriguing title of my film was, "Who Is Gary Gibo?". Gary had won the annual Ford Motor Company contest to find the best, the most talented Ford dealership employee in America. This interesting character was a Native American. Gary flew his own plane and had a great story to tell. This native of Hawaii also won a free trip . . . to the Bahamas!

In 1986 we invited Christa's father, Herbert, to live in our house on Bois Blanc Island. He didn't want to leave the Livonia home so Christa embarked on a plan only she would have envisioned. She duplicated his Livonia room in our island home. Not only his windows; his bookcases dropped right into the openings she now provided. She even built the interesting niche in the corner. Herbert came to the island. This was the exact room, the same as before in Livonia, but with a different view. He loved it. Lived there for 13 years.

Christa did not want her father to spend his first Thanksgiving celebration alone on Bois Blanc. She prepared a meal for him, and we traveled to the island. At 2:30 a.m. we were awakened by a phone call from our Livonia friend and neighbor who rented the house next door. She had terrible news. Our home was on fire. We immediately contacted Curt Plaunt, the Cheboygan ship's captain. He came at once in his own personal boat, took us across the water to town. And we drove south to Livonia.

As we parked at the end of our long driveway the Fire Marshall approached saying, "Ma'am, this is going to be difficult." We had lost four of our cats in that tragedy. Both the girls' bedrooms and ours had been trashed. Their school graduation photos were slashed. We also learned the firemen had initially run out of hose. They hadn't realized how deep the building was. Since the property was up for sale the Police Department detective wanted us to take a polygraph test. George Rizik, our lawyer, advised us to refuse and we did. We then asked George to negotiate the fire loss with our insurance company. He was very appreciative of the fact that we had given him complete authority.

George refused to settle for the paltry sum they offered. The actual settlement took a full year, but our attorney did a great job. His efforts paid off.

At one point the polyester-dressed insurance representative refused to accept the purchase price of a full-length raccoon coat destroyed by the fire. We met this investigator at the furrier's salon where Christa had purchased the coat only a month before. Of course, the furrier supported Christa.

We also spent weeks pouring through the remains of either fire damaged or destroyed household items. Christa and I researched and detailed the history and price of all items to support our claims. All this before the internet and the use of google. All the prices came from tedious research in the Sears catalogue. We continued the work until every item was accounted for though we were advised these remains were carcinogenic.

The center of the fire, Christa's edit suite. Her new Convergence was only a few months old.

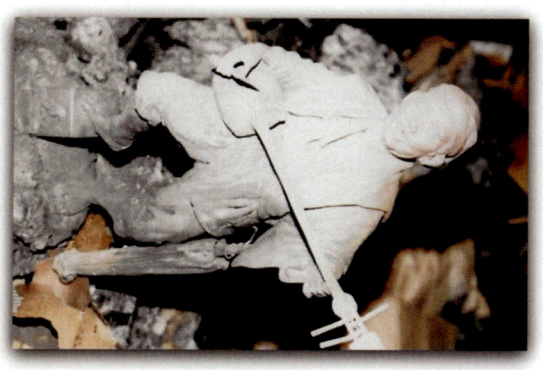

The Japanese Musician. Our treasured statue we hoped could be restored.

A STROKE OF LUCK

The editing bench, equipment, and jobs in process!

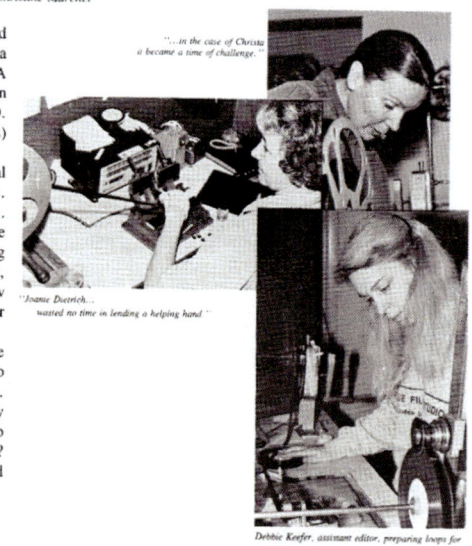

Detroit's Unique Support System
Media Community Rallies Behind Christa Kindt
by Christine Marchel

On November 28, 1986, Christa Kindt, a well-known and respected Detroit area film and videotape editor, experienced a tragic loss of her place of business, home, and equipment. A burglary and fire at Unique Film and Video, 34773 Seven Mile Road, Livonia, created damage estimated at $400,000. All those who know Christa and her cats (assistant editors) were touched by the death of four of these companions.

Every disaster of this type involves property and emotional damage. There is an inevitable dampening of the spirits. However, in the case of Christa it became a time of challenge. Shelter for the family was only the beginning. There was the need to deal with current client jobs, loss of her off-line editing suite and its videotape equipment, the film editing studio, horizontal KEM, and smoke-damaged film. Those who know Christa were not surprised at her response to these events, her display of courage, fortitude and perseverance.

None of us can survive disaster alone, and the immediate response of many is a tribute to Christa and our film/video community. She did not have to face the challenges alone. Besides the support of her producer/director husband, Shelby Newhouse, many individuals and companies stepped in to help. The community supported all of her efforts. The result? In a matter of days, Unique Film and Video was up and operating, able to meet her current client obligations.

What actually happened?

During the Thanksgiving Day holiday, Christa and her family were up north on Bois Blanc island. This was the first time in 15 years no one was at the studio or house overnight. The family was awakened at 4 a.m. by a phone call, made with care and understanding by Nancy Huckaby, a free-lance producer living next door.

Livonia's arson squad, fire marshall and a team of police detectives met Christa and her family when they arrived five hours later. The fire had started in the off-line editing salon during the course of a burglary. The damage was devastating.

What was the damage?

Ninety percent of the off-line equipment was fire damaged and could not be repaired. The KEM editing table and related items were a complete loss. At least 600, 3/4" cassettes were literally melted down, many records destroyed, film footage smoke damaged, three rooms charred and blackened, others totally smoke damaged. Christa, an animal lover, lost four of her eight cats.

We then purchased a parcel of land on the corner of Eight Mile Road and Cass in nearby Farmington Hills. Christa owned a small house that was also on the 14 acres where the Livonia home had stood. The farmer husband of a schoolteacher had built that house in 1943. We added an additional 100 feet to the purchased parcel and moved that house a distance of one mile.

CHANGES ALL AROUND

Living room, bed rooms, kitchen, and baths. Seven rooms on the move!

The mover was an interesting older man. He negotiated with Christa while looking at me. It was clear he was from the old school, couldn't look at her, couldn't negotiate with a woman. He stuck to his price and did an excellent job. Dishes that had been overlooked and were still in a cupboard remained intact after the move. They had not been damaged.

There was one incident that did result in damage. I was the culprit. A stranger had just seen me back up a 24-foot moving truck. I drove it right over our large flower box at the edge of our driveway. I then took off to turn around and try again. She shouted to Christa, "I have his license plate. I'll take it to the police!" Christa answered, "No problem. I've got his number too! He's my husband and when he comes home he'll need the police to protect him!" All this happened in the driveway of our Cass house.

We did some research and then commissioned the Ann Arbor architectural firm of Hobbs and Black to design an office building. One half of the building, which we called The Annex, would house Christa's editing suites, her 16 employees and my production office. The other half would be available for leasing. This was a perfect example of European wisdom and experience. Only Americans endure the challenges and costs of commuting. Christa came from a world where the owner of the business lived upstairs, downstairs, or next door. During the years we worked in the building we simply walked out of one door and into another. Commuting was for the birds. We were not birds!

A practical solution and a dream situation. Three years to completion.

Reception area of Unique Film and Video in The Annex. Marie Medlin, office manager, answers the phone. The fully restored Musician graces the corner of her desk!

CHANGES ALL AROUND

Christa ready to edit. On top of her world.

Christa worked closely with John Barker, the architect assigned to our project. He was a talented and good partner. Christa also designed an area for my son Dana within her studio. He's been doing what he should ever since. Composes scores for films and videotapes and writes songs. With only one exception Dana has scored all my films. Christa enjoyed every part of the Annex project, especially the moving and replanting of over 30 full-grown trees.

Around this time Phyllis, my first wife and mother of our children, had been living with Veda, her mother. They were drinking companions. After Veda died Phyllis was lonely and drinking by herself. Christa and I made two decisions in an effort to help. First, we provided a home for her in old Farmington. And Christa hired her as the receptionist in her studio. Since Phyllis never drove, we picked her up in the morning and dropped her off each evening. She now had a full day of interacting with others: employees, clients, our son Dana, and me. Her role at Unique was much more than just answering the telephone. She was a great cook. By 10:30 a.m. each morning the entire studio would smell of fresh banana bread! What a tease for the clients! They then had to wait until she finished preparing lunches for everyone. Here's evidence that wife and ex-wife can work together in harmony.

In 1997 the Michigan VUE magazine serving Michigan's Media Arts industry published a four-page article titled "Christa's Excellent Adventure." Christa reflected on 40 years in an ever-changing industry. David Gibbons, senior editor of the magazine wrote,

> She is a tall woman with a regal bearing. Yet, she's apt to giggle like a schoolgirl. At first glance, she appears staid and conservative; yet a closer look reveals something "arty." Dare I say "beat"? She is at the top of her very literate profession, and her clients and friends are among the most erudite. She is truly a liberated woman, who has neither little time nor much use for feminist politics. She works very hard, but always takes time to play with her numerous animal companions. She is, in short, a paradox. And, during the 40 years she's been here, Christa Kindt has become a beloved lion of the Detroit media.

An ill wind was blowing across miles of oxide coating. Film work was slowing. There was a new technology on the block. Clients began asking if Christa knew how to edit video. She quickly applies herself to learning the new medium.

Three years later, in November of 2000, an international organization of professionals who work in the field of videotape and film production convened an annual awards black tie dinner to announce winners in a variety of categories. The ITVA competition is fierce, and their awards coveted. The highlight of the evening is the announcement of the Legend of the Year. The person being honored is revealed through the playing of a short video produced for the occasion. This year's winner, CHRISTA KINDT: Legend of the Year 2000. The award says it all. "Christa Kindt: Your guidance, encouragement, leadership and integrity in the production industry have fostered these qualities in others." I would add, those who love her know this honor, deserved as it is, merely scratches the surface. Christa wrote of the use of technology and the future:

> Just because you can type, you're not a writer. Just because you can use the AVID you're not necessarily an editor. Because you can say action to somebody, you're not a director. It is an ever-changing industry. As an editor I have had a volume of productions in the past 10 years equal to the first 30 years, because of the speed with which I can now finish a one-hour show or commercial. If I project into the future, and I am planning to be part of that future, it will only get faster, better and more accessible to more people. I want to be part of it. I'm fascinated by it and I love it, and as long as it keeps me editing I'll be happy.

Christa predicted in five more years there would be no tape. It would all be digital.

MIRACLE OF THE DANCING SUN

Often, the history of acquiring a project and the making of the production can be fascinating. "Fatima" with Ricardo Montalban is a good example. Jean Whalen had never made a film or been involved with filmmaking. She was a devout Catholic and as a Marianist loving Mary, she wanted to advance the message of the Miracle of Fatima. While working as an executive assistant-secretary to the Sisters of Mercy, Jean formed the non-profit corporation St. Gabriel Media. Their board of directors included important members of Michigan's Catholic community. She then set out to produce a film about the Miracle of Fatima.

Her next step was to contact a co-religionist catholic producer in Hollywood. Jean was immediately given the West Coast treatment. Three men traveled to Lisbon, the capital of Portugal, ostensibly to find out what kind of equipment and facilities were available, survey locations, do some shooting, and plan the film. They returned after three weeks without an outline, treatment, or script. And what they had shot was not acceptable.

St. Gabriel Media was out $45,000. Joe Guimette, a friend of mine and vice-president of Anthony Franco's public relations firm was a member of Jean's Board of Directors. He suggested I be asked to study the film contract and counsel St. Gabriel Media. Sam Goldwyn once said, "A verbal contract isn't worth the paper it's written on." I thought of that saying as I studied the document. Jean had signed an agreement no experienced client would have accepted, written or verbal. I advised against keeping it. She next sought a Catholic producer in the Detroit market. I knew the producer she hired. He was experienced, honest, and capable of delivering a good product. Five thousand dollars later and with a treatment she found unacceptable, Jean again turned to her board member. Guimette informed St. Gabriel he'd resign from the board if I weren't hired to make the film. And that's how a nice agnostic Jewish boy got a devout Catholic client. Thomas O'Conner, a well-known Catholic writer, joined our team to assure that correct Catholic beliefs would always be present in any of the many passages I'd have to compose. Tom made a significant contribution to our final product for which I shall always be grateful. Our collaboration resulted in the hourlong Emmy Award-winning documentary "Fatima" narrated by Ricardo Montalban.

Again, the year was 1982. I had never heard of the Miracle of Fatima, nor had I been troubled by rumors of its "three secrets" and the catastrophic events they foretold. This production led to a journey into the past, a search for eye witnesses to the events of 1917 near a small village in Portugal, a priest's whispered instructions in confidence to help us reach Sister Lucia cloistered in a convent in Coimbra, the ancient capital of Portugal, and to a series of inexplicable coincidences which defy rational explanations.

After considerable research into the events of 1917 known as the Miracle of Fatima, I prepared a list of shooting locations and potential interviewees. These events refer to the visions of Mary, Mother of Christ, as reported by three shepherd children, Lucia and her cousins, Jacinta and Francisco. Our attempt to speak with Sister Lucia, lone survivor of the three children, was of paramount importance and would involve enormous amounts of time and effort.

One of those I interviewed in the U.S. was Doctor and historian Warren Carroll, President and founder of Christendom College, Front Royal, Virginia. He was among several who independently voiced the opinion our film project would never be completed since the devil would intervene. Or if it were completed, a terrible price would have to be paid.

An important part of Dr. Carroll's interview was his explanation of the role played by the mad monk Rasputin in the destruction of the Russian Monarchy and the death of the Czar and his family at the hands of the Bolsheviks. This story and its narrator were forcefully brought to mind by subsequent events. Anyone viewing the documentary can attest to the strength of Dr. Carroll's belief in the existence of evil as a tangible force to be reckoned with.

It wasn't long before I noticed an interesting phenomenon. Once they understood our mission, a number of people would ask that we be blessed. They not only wanted us to succeed. They were seeking divine intervention, wanted us protected. They had a deep belief in the existence of evil. I repeat: they wanted us protected.

Seventy thousand people were present at Fatima on Oct. 13, 1917, to witness the anticipated appearance of Mary. An unusual celestial event was reported. Newspapers wrote that the sun appeared to dance in the heavens. I contacted a NASA astrophysicist in an effort to see if there might be a scientist's explanation of this occurrence. Rather than have the interview at his office he invited me to join him for lunch at the Cosmos Club in Washington, DC. I'd never heard of this unique institution. It was a private social club incorporated in 1878 by men distinguished in science, literature, and the arts. Since its founding, the club has elected as members individuals who participate in virtually every profession that has anything to do with scholarship, creative genius, or intellectual distinction. Among its members have been three Presidents, two Vice Presidents, a dozen Supreme Court Justices, 32 Nobel Prize winners, 56 Pulitzer Prize winners, and 45 recipients of the Presidential Medal of Freedom. In June 1988 the club voted to welcome women as members.

I was told the appearance of the sun dancing in the sky could have been the result of a phenomenon called a perihelion. This would be due to the presence of certain active elements in the atmosphere. I also learned my host was both a scientist and a devoted Catholic. This was a rare and wonderful opportunity to be present among such distinguished company. I reported what I had learned to my client. However, I was refused permission to include the scientific possibility that the appearance of the sun's movement may have been the result of anything but a miracle.

I flew to Lisbon to continue my research and spent a week scouting locations for filming, arranging interviews, and locating historical photographs as well as other documents. The trip was not without its lighter moments and frustrations. The car rental firm presented me with a Mini Morris, designed to generate sympathy with the sardines of this world.

The Lisbon Airport was adjacent to the city's downtown district. I'd arrived at the height of Monday morning traffic. Every street was a racecourse with each experienced driver familiar with the track, driving flat out, and confident his or her life insurance was up to date. In retrospect, I'm sure some of the Portuguese words directed at me that morning would never be found in any Berlitz language course. My hotel reservation was at the Principe Real. In my effort to find the hotel I learned a significant fact regarding travel in Portugal. Portuguese are warm, friendly, and willing to help, but few speak English.

I soon found myself on a toll road taking me across a river and leaving the city. I paid the toll, left the road at the first opportunity, made the number of required turns to get my Mini Morris back on that road, but moving in the correct direction. After paying the toll again I finally decided on drastic action. I stopped a taxi, made him understand "Hotel Principe Real" and followed him to my destination. An inauspicious beginning! Early the next morning I was on my way to the village of Fatima and the Hotel Santa Maria. It was an exhilarating 90-mile continuation of the previous day's road race.

The irony of this 20th century Catholic miracle occurring next to a village bearing a Moslem name compelled me to examine its genesis. The explanation was simple and romantic. In the year 711 the Moors swept out of North Africa to conquer the Iberian Peninsula. Centuries later a grateful King honored one of the warriors who rid Portugal of the invaders by granting him land. The hero had fallen in love with a captured Moorish princess who bore the name of Mohammed's daughter, Fatima. He chose to venerate his bride and celebrate their marriage by christening a beautiful village in her name.

The clergy at the Basilica were expecting me, as was an American expatriate, all of whom were generous with their time and assistance. The community was made aware of my interest in locating eyewitnesses to the miracle of Fatima some 66 years earlier. Arrangements were made to film and interview two of Lucia's sisters, a sister-in-law, and a brother of Jacinta and Francisco. Cooperation was excellent and my list of shots was growing.

Note that as a child Sister Lucia and her two cousins had seen Mary at Fatima on the 13th of May, June, July, August, and September of 1917. Seventy thousand people were on hand on October 13 to test the children's story. It was shortly after noon when the "Miracle of the Sun" took place.

Wherever I went, with whomever I met, I explored the possibility of an interview with Sister Lucia. Father Luciano Guerra, Rector of the Fatima Basilica, and Monsignor Jose Galamba de Oliveira, a 1917 witness and interrogator of Sister Lucia, were sympathetic but unable to help. An American Cardinal was using his contacts with the Vatican, but to no avail. Then I was taken aside by a priest who asked to remain anonymous. My informant said he'd disclose a possible route to Sister Lucia, but I was never to reveal the source of my information. My pursuit of Sister Lucia was beginning to resemble an international mystery by John le Carré. In a rather conspiratorial way, the priest told me the sister's secretary and confidant, the Marquesa de Cadaval, widow of a prominent nobleman, lived in a Lisbon suburb. I should speak with her.

My spirits soared. I tracked down the telephone number and for the next three days and at every opportunity placed telephone calls to her home. Each time we were connected the person answering could only speak Portuguese. I was unable to make myself understood. Finally, shortly before leaving Fatima for Lisbon, I reached the Marquesa's daughter, who did speak English. She told me her mother the Marquesa had left the day before to visit her family in Venice, Italy. Calls to Venice proved to be a replay of my efforts in Portugal except this time the language at the other end of the line was Italian!

Returning to Lisbon I visited the reference room of a leading newspaper, purchased several historical items, and researched the government's collection of records, documents, and photographs. Many of the pictures were excellent. I made a large selection. They said the photos I'd ordered would take some time to reproduce but would be forwarded to my office in the United States. My offer to pay was refused since this Portuguese Republic was a socialistic nation. All I requested would be free. True to their word about a month later the package arrived.

Saturday, April 23, 1983, I departed Lisbon for London where my crew who were flying in from the States would join me. John Holmstrom my Director of Photography would be in from Los Angeles. He'd be joined by our second camera operator Dr. Edwin Rennell Jr. (an oral surgeon), as well as Bill Coe, Assistant Cameraman, and Sheldon Nueman our Sound Recordist. These crew members came from Michigan. It was time for another stroke of luck. I needed to pick up a gaffer, an electrician. He'd be a very critical member of my team responsible for the placement of all lights. Who did the London union assign to Shelby Newhouse? Who was available to join this small documentary crew? Derek Gatrell. He had been the gaffer on Barbara Streisand's award winning "Yentl" as well as the wonderful film, "Chariots of Fire." Derek would drive one van and John Holmstrom the other. John's first action was the printing of a sign. He hung this at the rear of his vehicle. Clearly, he'd been in England before. It read: Danger: American Driver.

After checking in at the St. Ermines Hotel I immediately called Venice seeking the Marquesa de Cadaval. Once again, my command of Italian proved inadequate. I shared my frustration with the desk clerk. No problem, he said. The chef in charge of the hotel's kitchen was from Italy. A short time later the chef and I were placing another call to Venice. Of course, when the Marquesa was summoned to the phone she spoke impeccable English. Using whatever powers of persuasion I possess I stated our case, which was to produce a film to advance the message of Fatima. Clearly, Sister Lucia's participation would provide the single most important element we could hope for since the sister was the principal figure in the Fatima story. The Marquesa de Cadaval listened politely, asked several questions, and then gently explained that she had made a pact with Sister Lucia years before never to use their friendship in this fashion. She could not ask her to consent to an interview. That would be unthinkable. I had to respect her wishes. So that chapter in our effort to reach the elusive Lucia ended in our London hotel room. We remain convinced the Vatican chooses for reasons of their own, to protect Sister Lucia from visitors and to let her memoirs and published reports of interrogations stand alone.

Our most fascinating interview took place in a cottage in Robertsbridge, England. The subject was Malcolm Muggeridge, an octogenarian, philosopher, iconoclast, former journalist, and broadcaster who, several years earlier at the age of 80, converted to Catholicism. No one was spared his pithy erudite views on the state and fate of the western world. Malcolm more than lived up to his reputation as the man thrown off the BBC, the result of his comments directed at the Royal Family, particularly the Queen Mother. From more than 40 minutes of pure Muggeridge, all of which reads like carefully crafted prose, we excerpted those gems that appear in the documentary.

The crew's journey to Portugal included traveling with 31 boxes of equipment, film stock, and personal baggage. As any seasoned producer will tell you, preparation is the key to a smooth production. Relaxed and confident that each "T" had been crossed and each "I" had been dotted, I waited for British Customs to arbitrarily select the cases they'd choose to open and inspect. Most civilized countries in the world are signatories to an international convention. It recognizes the carnet as the primary document for moving goods across borders with a minimum of paper work and delays. I'd executed a carnet before leaving for Europe and left several pages of explicit instructions on how it was to be handled. We were now advised by very pleasant but firm British Customs Officers at Heathrow Airport that the boxes arrayed before them, which they were preparing to inspect did not, in fact, exist since our crew had failed to get the carnet signed by a U.S Customs Officer when leaving the States. British Customs was correct. Technically these goods had never even entered the country. Ultimately, common sense prevailed, and we fared better with customs than with the Marquesa de Cadaval.

Our flight to Portugal was uneventful. Two Mercedes Benz diesel vans proved more than adequate for the next leg of our journey. With the Santa Maria hotel in Fatima as our base of operations we proceeded to shoot interviews and additional material, which would provide visual support to various aspects of the story. Our stars must have been arranged in a perfect orbit. The following was unbelievable. Successful arrangements had been made to film at the cloistered convent in Coimbra where Sister Lucia actually lived. Arriving at the convent we took notice of graffiti on the outside wall. Its translation reflected the anti-clerical views of several political groups vying for power in the national elections of that year. The graffiti appears in our film. It reads , "Religion is the opium of the People."

Our translator Father George knocked on the convent's wooden door. After a brief wait an opening appeared as a small transom slid into its recessed chamber. The sister assigned to greet visitors that day listened to the explanation of our visit, closed the transom and disappeared. After several minutes an older nun appeared. She politely and pleasantly exchanged words with Father George and proceeded to open the door inviting our crew and equipment inside. We learned how unusual such a visit was. Only a priest hearing confession or a medical doctor would normally be permitted contact with the convent nuns. However, we were allowed to re-enact a scene in the chapel with one of the sisters as long as we did not reveal her face.

The following was very important to our story. Our research revealed Sister Lucia had spent many months assisting an artist as he created a statue of Mary. This work was done as an attempt to recreate the Mother of Jesus as she appeared in the vision seen by Sister Lucia as a child in 1917. She's reported to say it's a good likeness. This is the very chapel where that statue stands. That information assured its appearance in our documentary. The opportunity to enter and work in this environment was unexpected and truly welcomed.

SECRETS AND THE CURSE

As we approach the subject of the secrets of Fatima it may help to recall the visit of Pope John Paul II to Germany in 1980. A small group was allowed to meet with him privately at Fulda. One of their questions concerned the third secret of Fatima. Our Lady shared these secrets with the children during the Fatima visitations in 1917. Years later, Sister Lucia had presented this information, these secrets to her superiors. They in turn had sent her letter on to the Vatican. The first two secrets had been made known to the world. They had to do with visions of hell. Here is a translation from Chiesa Viva, October 1981. This is a monthly ecclesiastical review published in Italy. It carried the story of His Holiness' visit to Germany.

Questioner: "Holy Father, what about the 'secret' of Fatima, which was to be published in 1960"?

Holy Father's reply: "On account of its deeply disturbing contents and to avoid giving world communist powers occasion for certain interferences, my predecessors preferred a 'diplomatic account' of the secret. Besides, every Christian should be satisfied to know what follows."

> When we read (in the secret) that the oceans will flood entire continents, that men will be deprived of life all of a sudden, from one minute to the next, and this by the millions, when people know this, it is indeed unnecessary to insist on the publication of the secret. Many want to know only out of curiosity and sensation. They however forget that 'knowing' carries also responsibility with it. All they want is to satisfy their curiosity. This is dangerous when, at the same time, men are unwilling to do anything about it, saying that after all it is of no use!

At this point the Pope took hold of his Rosary saying, "Here is the medicine against this evil! Pray, pray and put no further questions. Recommend all the rest to Our Lady."

Aware of intense world-wide interest in the third secret, of rumors of pending cataclysmic, catastrophic events destined to befall mankind, we'd arranged an interview with the Bishop of Leiria-Fatima, Don Alberto Cosme do Amaral, at his Palace in Coimbra. Bishop do Amaral had interrogated Sister Lucia and I eagerly awaited his response to our questions. We arrived at the Palace and were immediately informed that the bishop would agree to our filmed interview only after I signed a contract. We learned that shortly before our arrival an interview had appeared in the Italian press that purported to be between the author and Bishop do Amaral. It included extensive quotations attributed to the bishop. That interview was a complete fabrication. It had never taken place. Fearful of being misquoted, the bishop insisted on an agreement guaranteeing his right to review a transcript of our interview before the documentary was released. First, I was shown the room in which we would film the bishop. A chair was selected and while my crew set up the lights and two cameras, I retired to his office, sat at a typewriter, and composed a short contract granting him the right of review. It was taken to him, translated, agreed to, and executed.

Bishop Don Alberto Cosme do Amaral, me, and the mystery chair. (left)

When I returned with the bishop, I was surprised to see a different chair had been lit. It was not the one I had chosen. The one that had been selected could not be seen. There was no time to question my crew and we began the interview.

In 1942, the writings of Sister Lucia, including the secret in a separate envelope, were sent to the Bishop of Leiria-Fatima. In 1957, 15 years later, those writings were forwarded to Rome. Pope John opened the envelope, read its contents, and kept it secret. Each subsequent Pope was given the letter containing the secret. As seen in the film, here is Bishop do Amaral's response to my question concerning this subject of such universal and acute interest.

> In many parts of the world, in different countries, many versions of the secret of Fatima have appeared. I have often received stories and articles published in newspapers and magazines concerning the secret written as if the author knew the secret. There were so many I decided to contact Sister Lucia myself. Because these stories describe apocalyptic events, tell of disgraces that will befall humanity, of nations that will disappear, including descriptions of actual contemporary political situations that we are experiencing, I felt it was my duty as the present Bishop of Leiria-Fatima, as someone responsible for the authenticity of the message, it was my duty to clarify it. Sister Lucia said that nothing like this was mentioned in these supernatural communications that she

received. In any event, we know the message of Fatima. It is enough to change our life. The message of Fatima is enough. It moves us to continue our contribution to the salvation of our society. And this is what is important.

It was the last day of our stay in Fatima. As I paid our hotel bill late that afternoon and was talking with the manager of the Santa Maria, I expressed my disappointment at not finding more eyewitnesses to the 1917 events. Shortly afterwards he appeared accompanied by a young bus boy we'd seen working in the dining room. The boy spoke no English, but we learned his grandparents told him of being present Oct. 13, 1917, when the Miracle of the Sun had occurred. Our crew and equipment were quickly assembled. Father Paul, our translator, was located. We set out to find the farm of Manuel Pereira and Maria Augusta Frazão. They were wonderful! It was clear they'd never before been questioned about Fatima and were eager to tell their story. They were totally unaware of the camera, lights, or Shel Nueman lying on the ground at their feet pointing a microphone at them. They were unaffected by it all and appeared to be delighted at the presence of gathering neighbors who came to see what was going on. We were shooting in their farmyard sharing the space with the family's goats. The elderly farmer and his wife sat under the roof of a shed, while we filmed from the outside. Neither the onset of darkness nor rain slowed them down. We got one of the best sequences in the film. Before we left, Maria went into the farmhouse and came out with a small photo of herself taken when she was younger, perhaps 70. She insisted on giving me the picture and a kiss, both of which I treasure.

Note the following event and the date. The Pope was being driven in his Pope mobile through a crowd of about 20,000 worshippers in Rome when four bullets struck him. Many of those who witnessed the shooting in the crowded square burst into tears or screamed and fell to their knees in disbelief. It was May 13, 1981. The anniversary of the Miracle of Fatima. A significant date for Pope John Paul II. He credited Sister Lucia's visions with saving his life.

Sister Lucia de Jesus Rosa dos Santos was an icon to devout Catholics everywhere. She was one of their church's most influential women of the 20th century and a close friend of Pope John Paul II. Sister Lucia had been deaf, blind, and ailing for several years when she died in her room in the Carmelite convent of Santa Teresa in the city of Coimbra. The very convent I had visited. She had lived there since 1948. The date of her death was Feb. 13, 2005. She was 97 years of age.

As we were departing Portugal, customs officers separated those of us departing for the U.S. from our British crew member, Derek. Our train was ready to leave for the airport when Derek came running to the barrier between us shouting. I had neglected to sign his check! He pushed it through the fence; I quickly signed it thereby saving my reputation should I ever have to return to filmmaking in the British Isles. And restoring his confidence in American producers.

The time has come to reveal my secret of Fatima, really of Coimbra. While I was engaged in preparing that contract for the bishop's signature my crew broke the ornate chair that had been selected for the bishop's interview. They managed to put it together and hide it before I returned and made sure we selected a different chair for the bishop when he arrived. There was no time for discussion. We had to proceed with the interview. This secret was revealed to the world and this producer about 40,000 feet over the Atlantic on our return flight to the States.

Christa, my wonderful partner, film editor, and wife assembled the results of our European trip along with the material I shot in the United States with cameraman Barry Meier. Jean Whalen, my client, asked Catholic writer Tom O'Connor to study my script guaranteeing that in all respects it conformed to Catholic teaching. He was great to work with.

My son, Dana, not only composed an original symphonic score for "FATIMA," but also conducted the orchestra. Postproduction was soon completed. Jean Whalen and the world had her film.

St. Gabriel Media quickly sold almost 45,000 "FATIMA" cassettes. Television time had been purchased and the program appeared in 71 cities across America, often in prime time. Among those cities were Chicago, Los Angeles, Detroit, and Philadelphia. "FATIMA" was also awarded an Emmy. Pope John Paul II saw the film and invited Jean Whalen to attend an audience at the Vatican. The Holy Father told Jean how important the film was. That it was one of the best catholic documentaries ever made and asked if it could be produced in Spanish. Of course, the answer was yes.

We had the script translated. I traveled to New York to cast the 19 Spanish-speaking actors for the voice-over parts. We then returned to Los Angeles where Ricardo Montalban did a repeat performance, only this time in his first language, Spanish. And as before, his work was a gift. Even the $5,000 offered as a thank you was declined. The Spanish version appeared on television in Latin America, Central America, and Spain. English-speaking countries have aired the production in Europe, Australia, and New Zealand.

As I write these words Pope John Paul II has died and been beatified without the customary five-year wait after his death. The next step is Sainthood.

This was a film some thought should not be undertaken. Dire predictions had been made, but now it was an accomplished fact. Three events occurred which I'll recount. The first may be characterized as having modest monetary significance. The other two bear metaphysical signs you may interpret for yourself.

Filming the Spanish version of "Fatima" in California. Ricardo Montalban, Christa, and Script Supervisor rehearse dialogue while crew sets up.

Some may argue there is no more commercial geographical location in the United States than Southern California. I, however, have a story that betrays that image. When organizing the Los Angeles filming of Ricardo's Spanish narration, I contacted a Hollywood caterer of film shoots to arrange for the feeding of my crew. We'd never done business with this company, and they advised us the minimum number of persons they'd feed was 25. Our group numbered only 13. Then for some unaccountable reason the caterer said, "Don't worry about it. We'll take care of your needs and there will be no charge." Members of our sophisticated, experienced California crew were made aware of this arrangement while enjoying an outstanding lunch. They found it hard to believe. What would they have thought of these next two occurrences?

Christa and I were flying to New York to audition and record those Spanish-speaking actors. She called my attention to the man seated in the row ahead of me. Something he was reading had caught her eye. She saw the name "Fatima" on the open page of his book, but that was all she could make out. I moved to the seat beside him, introduced myself, explained the purpose of our trip and asked what he was reading. He was reading the story of Fatima in

Spanish! The next day in the recording studio while I was directing our Spanish-speaking cast Christa had occasion to carry a message to the receptionist in the lobby. The receptionist was reading a book. A book I had in my library. A book Christa had seen me use during the writing of the script. It was a biography by Alex De Jonge, "THE LIFE AND TIMES OF GRIGORII RASPUTIN," the mad monk. The juxtaposition of a stranger reading the story of Fatima in Spanish as we worked on the Spanish version and the studio receptionist reading the same book I'd used to research the history of the mad monk appears compelling. At least enough to make one's spine tingle. It's as if a message is being communicated, but I confess its contents and source remain a mystery to me. The rational answer is coincidence.

Historian William H. Carroll was convinced the project would not be finished or if it were there would be a price to be paid. Two notes: It was after the completion of this documentary we experienced the disastrous burning of our home and studio. In addition to the destruction, the physical and financial repercussions, and the heartbreaking loss of our four cats, this 1986 fire was responsible for the loss of irreplaceable reels of film. Some were actually on the KEM editing machine in our home. These reels represented footage remaining from the number of religious films I had been shooting. I'd envisioned a project that would use this material and called it "Return to God." They disappeared in the fire. However, if one chooses to make the leap that the fire was in any way related to "Fatima" it was a modest cost. Jean Whalen, our client and President of St. Gabriel Media, lost her 31-year-old daughter. She took her own life. Within two years, Jean died of cancer.

Purchasers of the film, "FATIMA" received both the film and the following text:

1917: The First World War is raging in Europe; millions are dying on the Western Front. Russia is poised on the brink of the Bolshevik Revolution. And in a small village of Portugal a beautiful lady appears to three young shepherd children. Fatima stands as a spiritual harbor, a refuge for pilgrims, a way to God. It presents a sobering warning and a message of hope to the world.

Clips from the Warner Brothers film on Fatima re-enact the events from the first appearance of Our Lady on 13 April 1917 to the phenomenon of The Dancing Sun on 13 October 1917. Film footage of World War I and other powerful visuals create the context of Ricardo Montalban's convincing narrative. The documentary also features on-location footage and expert commentary by Malcolm Muggeridge,

Alexander Solzhenitsyn, James Hitchcock, and Warren Carroll.

"FATIMA," Produced by St. Gabriel Media. This one-hour-long television documentary has been rated by some as one of the best Catholic documentaries ever made. "FATIMA" is perhaps the greatest single contribution to the Catholic film world to date; a rare combination of sound content with superb cinematic quality.

Trinity Communications.

OMNE TRIUM PERFECTUM ...
Good Things Come in Threes

In the late 1980s the Ford Motor Company and the UAW had a joint committee on quality control. The advertising agency representing this committee hired me to produce a film that showed all the steps required to make an automobile. The film's title said it all, "From Drawing Board to Delivery." We were asked to film the various stages of manufacturing at the old historic River Rouge facility. I have great respect for working men and women who labor on production lines. Today their products reach the ends of the earth. I welcomed the opportunity to produce a tribute to those who labor in the automotive industry.

My son Kim wrote an outstanding script. I developed a budget and presented this to my client. His response was something I had never heard before. "You have more money to spend on this project." Well, that was an easy request to fulfill. More sophisticated equipment could be employed, a helicopter scheduled and we could shoot with 35mm film stock instead of the typical 16mm used for most industrial films. I made adjustments, resubmitted the new budget, and it was approved by my client.

Virtually every automotive film most of us had been making for years and years concentrated on advances in automation. This project gave me the opportunity to show more than machines. I was able to film people, actual human beings immersed in their work. They were not aware of my crew, the camera, or me. These workers were engaged in what they were doing. Their job! Christa loved the footage.

The film was submitted to two festivals. It was returned by the first. They said it was too much like a feature film. The quality exceeded the typical industrial film. It wouldn't be fair to other contestants. The second festival organization disagreed. They accepted "From Drawing Board to Delivery." Our film won a GOLD Medal from the New York International Film Festival.

Reye's Syndrome? I'd never heard of it. Yet, this deadly disease led to the most emotional shoot of my career. Reye's strikes swiftly and without warning. It can attack any child, teen, or young adult. All body organs are affected and death may quickly ensue. The National Reye's Syndrome Foundation asked me to produce a documentary to create public awareness of this danger.

I interviewed and filmed leading experts. Reye's was first recognized clinically in 1929. By 1971 investigations revealed the inevitable involvement of the liver. In 1980 the account of an association between aspirin and Reye's was published in the journal Pediatrics. In 1982 the Public Health Service report definitely linked aspirin exposure to Reye's syndrome. Reye's has a very rapid onset, and early diagnosis is key to surviving the illness. Unfortunately, there are still unknown mysterious factors in the Reye's syndrome disease. Aspirin is not always present or required for the development of Reye's. But look at the odds. Ninety percent of cases are associated with the use of either aspirin or other Salicylates.

Our client arranged interviews with two sets of parents. Each couple had lost a 3-year-old child one year before we filmed their story. I was soon crying while shooting. My crew members were also in tears. I needed to interview physicians who had lost Reye's patients and I was concerned that these doctors might not agree to an interview. I need not have worried. They wanted to help. Each one I approached agreed to appear. A transcript of all the sound tracks was made and we met with our clients, John and Terri Freudenberger. They'd organized the National Reye's Syndrome Foundation since losing their daughter to this disease.

After I read our script to them, John asked if this was just a story I'd written? No, I said. The interviewees had spoken everything I'd read word for word. We were asked to complete the film. Their foundation immediately ordered 1,000 prints and sent a copy to each of their chapters. If you are a parent, I hope you'll commit the following to memory.

After a viral illness an individual should be watched for these symptoms during the next two or three weeks. They usually occur in this order:

Relentless or continuous vomiting

Listlessness (loss of pep, energy, with little interest in their environment)

Drowsiness (excessive sleepiness)

Personality change (such as irritability, slurred speech, sensitivity to touch)

Disorientation or confusion (unable to identify family members, whereabouts, or answer questions)

Combativeness (striking out at those trying to help them)

Delirium (convulsions, or loss of consciousness)

"Reye's Syndrome: A Real and Present Danger" won a CINE Golden Eagle Award, Golden Cassette Award and an Honorary Mention Certificate in the Columbus Video and Film Festival.

Who was Charles Stewart Mott? He was a member of General Motor's board of directors for 60 years. The largest single stockholder. Mr. Mott was also a major philanthropist with a deep interest in children's health and education. In 1965, the Charles Stewart Mott Foundation donated $6.5 million as a grant to improve the existing pediatric division within the Department of Internal Medicine through the University of Michigan Health System in Ann Arbor, Michigan. In 2005, the Foundation gave an additional $25 million toward the construction of a new facility. The children's hospital is consistently ranked as one of the top pediatric centers in the nation. Ruth Rawlings Mott, his widow, was interested in the production of a documentary film about her late husband and Applewood, their Flint, Michigan estate.

A number of prospective filmmakers were interviewed. Anyone fortunate enough to win this commission would have one of the wealthiest families in America as their client. Think of it this way: filmmakers all over this country were prepared to sacrifice their eye teeth. Christa and I were summoned and traveled to Flint. Paul Yeager, head of the financial affairs office of the Charles Stewart Mott family, interviewed us. Both Mr. Yeager and a banker met us in a room on the 18th floor of the tallest building in the city, the Mott Building. With their unlimited resources I was certain whoever got the job would be scrutinized as though they were seeking a national security clearance.

Some things in life progress slowly. We heard nothing for a year and assumed someone else got the job. We were elated when a call came from Flint to visit again and make a second presentation. There were subsequent meetings. Then the writing of a contract that would extend over the period of a year since Mrs. Mott wanted her gardens to be viewed in all four seasons. I began what for me is probably the most interesting part of my work, researching the subject. This included preparation of a list of potential interviewees, family members, documents, automotive archives, historical automotive literature, and The Detroit News and Detroit Free Press morgues. I conducted a series of pre-interviews. Barry Meier was the best cameraman for this film. He had all the qualities I'd look for as my Director of Photography. Barry is a sensitive cinematographer, a good operator with his own film equipment, the ability to comport himself appropriately given the social circumstances, and we enjoyed working together.

An outstanding crew was assembled, and we began filming a series of interviews, including several lengthy sessions with Ruth Mott. She was in her 80s and her mind was clear and sharp, memory and vocabulary excellent. Transcripts of the interviews were prepared, and I wrote the script. Christa and I met with Ruth and I read the script to her. She was delighted and asked me to proceed with the next stage.

Now the challenge was to find visual support for what I'd written. Permission was given to study all the family photo albums. What a treasure! Then another stroke of luck! I found voice recordings of Mr. Mott as well as film of the two of them at lunch on the patio and color film of an interview with our subject when he was in his 90s.

Filming an interview with Ruth Mott. Director of Photography Barry Meier behind the camera.

The estate enjoyed a well-deserved reputation for its gardens and greenhouse. One of our efforts to capture its beauty required some mathematics and precision of execution. We filmed the garden at each of the four seasons that year. The camera was placed at the same location and height and then panned at the same speed. As the seasons changed Christa dissolved each of the four takes into the next. Ruth also knew there would be tours of Applewood after her death. So she requested the production of a short video for use as an introduction to these tours.

We had footage revealing the wonderful sense of humor enjoyed by Charles Stewart Mott. He and several others were participating in the funeral service of a mutual friend. After noting that the deceased had been 89 years of age, they discussed their own respective ages. On learning each was approaching that milestone, Mott suggested maybe it was a waste of time to go home.

There are many great stories demonstrating Mr. Mott's penny-pinching attitude. He would wear a pencil down to its nub. The story I like best was told to me by his son. Stewart noticed the rug in his father's office had several holes. It was wearing out. Each morning he and his father would attend a business meeting after which they'd be joined by several others and would leave for lunch. This day Mott excused himself and said he'd see them after they returned. When they came back Stewart discovered why his dad had disappeared. He'd bought a can of paint that matched the color of the rug and had painted the floor in those areas where the rug had worn out!

JIMMY, HERBERT, AND THE ISLAND

"Here Kitty, Kitty, here Kitty"! Alan Dietrich, tanked up pretty good, had gotten out of his car to address the white fur on the side of the street. Al picked it up, placed it on the front seat, and continued on his way home. It was the evening before Easter and whoever had deposited this bundle must have intended it as an Easter present.

Monday morning Al's mother Joanie took her son's gift to work. Joanie was the negative cutter in Christa's editing studio. Christa welcomed whatever it was. Remember, when we married she had 12 cats and two dogs. Any animal was something to be loved. Guess what Alan had found in his drunken stupor? Not a kitty. A rooster! Christa immediately named it Jimmy.

It was love at first sight. They were made for each other, Jimmy's head tucked beneath Christa's chin, snuggled up, in love. For months Jimmy could be seen perched in the tree adjacent to the window through which he could observe her editing. Though outside he truly had a ringside seat. Patiently waiting for her to come out and play, that rooster became another member of our family. We took him to Insel Haus where he became the master of his own household. Yes, we provided chickens. Let's face it. Jimmy had a harem. Now Christa's father Herbert had a source of fresh eggs!

But there's more. As much as Jimmy adored Christa, he was mad about Mike Gahn. Mad as in hate, angry, as in holding a death wish for Mike our permanent employee. That rooster had a plan. A military maneuver. He executed it and Mike found himself to be a patient at Cheboygan's hospital. Jimmy sinking his talon into Mike's calf necessitated that trip to town. Biologists tell us there is such a thing as imprinting. Jimmy knew Christa was his mother; I'm convinced it goes both ways. Evidence may be seen on Insel Haus' exterior stair railings. Yes, those are paintings of Jimmy the Rooster.

Thinking back now to our first meeting with Jimmy, I can't believe my calendar! We are all aging. My first wife Phyllis experienced a major operation after which she was enrolled in a nursing home. Christa and I would often visit. Phyllis introduced us to the other residents as, "This is my husband and this is his wife." The nursing home staff and those in their care were always delighted to see us since we'd often bring Teddy Bear, our wonderful dog. He loved everyone and the feeling was mutual. The year was 1998. As we were driving off after visiting Phyllis, we received a phone call on our car phone. It was Graham Whipple, deputy sheriff on Bois Blanc Island. Christa's father, Herbert, who had been living in our island home for 13 years, had died from a massive heart attack. I conducted the simple service held for Herbert at the island's Coast Guard Chapel. All members of the family attended including Christa's brother Klaus, who lives with his wife Angele in San Diego. Herbert had served in the German navy in World War II. I'd served in the American infantry. We had never talked about the war. He did what he had to do. I did what I had to do. We never spoke of the tragic period of antisemitism and the inhuman acts perpetuated during the Hitler era. The Nazis didn't invent antisemitism. They were simply the first to organize it so it could be used as an effective weapon of the state.

Some of the residents on the island were aware I'd been involved in broadcasting in Detroit, but they knew few details of my career. Of course rumors quickly developed in this small town atmosphere. I was said to be known as "the Voice of Detroit." This would have been news to everyone else in the Detroit media, but I do think it contributed to my election to the township board as a trustee the following year.

Service on this five-person board has been very interesting. At one meeting I suggested Bois Blanc might benefit from having an ombudsman. Someone shouted out from the audience, "What kind of a woodsman is that?"

I knew that guy could do a dozen things I couldn't do. I just dropped the idea.

After 10 years I resigned from the board in 2009. There is a difference in the culture of the north as opposed to that of the south of Michigan. I'm not addressing the sense of morality or ethics. Good and bad exist everywhere. But sometimes the contrasts can be striking.

For example. How does one do business on this island? A builder has his crew working on our house. Inside the plumber is adding shower number nine to our living quarters. Christa told the plumber he could have our 1987 GMC truck by reducing whatever we will owe for his work. That truck only has a couple hundred thousand miles on it. The builder hears about the deal she's made and reminds her that about 13 years ago when Christa's dad died, she'd told him when that truck is available you can buy it.

The plumber says, "Christa, look, I can see you forgot. Let him have the truck."

The builder turns to the plumber and says, "You live in town. Whenever you're on the island and need a truck you can have it . . . for a dollar a day."

Smiles all around! It was time to check the truck's license plate. Guess what? The plate was for 2010. This is 2012!

The builder spoke with our island's deputy sheriff who said, "You can drive it, but you have to get a new plate within two weeks." No, they never heard of the word bureaucracy on this island. They don't even want to know how to spell it.

This story must be called "Save The Fox's Den." Brent Sharpe is our township supervisor. He has a construction business and is currently working on Insel Haus. A small historic structure on our property is called The Fox's Den. Everyone on Bois Blanc Island knows it is home to a fox that rears her young each spring. It provides great fun to all when they can observe the youngsters romping around, chasing each other like puppies. And at this stage they aren't red, but grey.

Early last century there was a lumber mill

The Fox's Den. Possibly another restoration project for Christa.

near the beach in front of the building. This structure was probably home for the mill's supervisor. Over the last 75 years it has fallen into disrepair. There have been no complaints from Mrs. Fox, but Christa would like to see it restored. Brent Sharpe sees the wisdom in this request and has agreed to help. This will undoubtedly be an undertaking every island resident will approve of. It will also be a test to see if Mrs. Fox has a sense of history.

Today was graduation day, the end of the school year for those four students in attendance at our island's one-room schoolhouse. Please note that at times we have only one student. You will always know if that's the case. As you drive by, you'll see a cement block tied to the end of our seesaw. Today's program opened with the pledge of allegiance. The four youngsters were holding a large paper American flag they'd made. This was followed by a second pledge:

> I pledge allegiance to the flag of Michigan,
> And to the state for which it stands,
> Two beautiful peninsulas united by a bridge of steel,
> Where equal opportunity
> And justice to all is our ideal.

Where on earth, but on this tiny island could one witness and indeed participate in such an occasion? There must have been 85 islanders in attendance. The frequent applause was thunderous. The most solemn moment was when the one graduate, dressed in the appropriate black cap and gown and wearing tennis shoes, walked down the aisle between the rows of those in attendance. He reached the mike and read his eighth-grade commencement address. He spoke of his family, his teacher who happened to be his mother, and talked about his great-grandfather, the 91-year-old retired captain of our ferry who of course was in today's audience. Next year George Spray our graduate would attend high school in Cheboygan, five miles across the water. He'd live on the mainland with relatives and return each weekend to visit his folks on the island.

The 6-year-old daughter of our postmaster gave an unforgettable reading. Clearly a grade A student. Yes, it was an Off-Broadway show. The graduate's younger brother, another one of the four students, came through with an arresting performance. Each member of the cast read a short story and then explained it's moral. No church sermon could have been more inspirational.

This was all worth the price of admission. Bring a plate to pass. The four students made every media mistake in the books. It was wonderful! Cues missed, slide film tilted, out of focus, off mike readings, too loud, too low, recorded music started, stopping, started again. Larry, president of the school board, read his address. He is the owner of Hawk's Landing, our island's combined country store and restaurant. He was not wearing his usual t-shirt and baseball cap. It was the first time I'd seen him wearing a shirt and tie. This outgoing gregarious man whom we all knew, was uncomfortable but unforgettable. Members of the school board also came to the front and embraced our graduate. At the conclusion there was food and a beautiful enormous cake! There was no doubt this was a never-to-be-forgotten affair. Our school's teacher holds a teaching certificate and is amazingly gifted. If history is any precursor of what the future may bring, I'm proud to note our island's supervisor was born on Bois Blanc Island, attended this school, and today holds a doctorate in chemistry. Obviously, the student to teacher ratio is somehow related to this good educational record.

On occasion life on Bois Blanc Island can be hazardous. We deliver our garbage bags to the transfer station and toss our burnable cardboard and wooden boxes into the huge burner. When tossing them into the fire a blowback occurred. Christa singed her eyebrows and hair. It was not a disaster, but they took weeks to return to normal.

One of our builder's projects is to restore a marvelous weather vane to the peak of our roof. The weather vane looks like a large sailing ship. This is the third effort to attach it. It hasn't been able to remain aloft after being battered by offshore winds. This third try will face wind from a different direction. I told our friend the builder I'd hold him responsible if this one doesn't make it, if wind takes it down. His reply, "If there's a tsunami, sue me!" This kind of banter is another reason to live, work and die here.

Another builder, Wayne Price from Harrison, Michigan, unwittingly played a major role in our Bois Blanc Island history. This unprincipled, fast-talking builder introduced several ideas designed to generate projects he could undertake on this virtually undeveloped island. First, he convinced us to engage the services of a survey firm to delineate parcels of our land we could then offer for sale.

Five of our waterfront parcels were on the Straits of Mackinac. The secluded character and privacy of Insel Haus was protected since any structure, even if built on the nearest lot, could not be seen from the house. Our Bed and Breakfast home now stood on 127 acres. A little more than a mile south of the waters of the Straits, our property included four waterfront Lake Thompson lots and two interior pieces of property.

Wayne Price engineered the sale of Lake Thompson lot #2 to auto dealer Dave Fernelius. Certainly a stroke of luck! Our bank took $25,000 significantly reducing our mortgage. While Christa was editing a film in Farmington Hills, I sold Lake Thompson lot #4 to Judge Steve Sheridan of Saugatuck, Michigan.

Wily Wayne Price also noticed a huge gravel pit that no longer had gravel. It had been worked over for years by our wonderful neighbors, Ray and Beverly Dalby. Wayne suggested that vein of gravel might continue across a two-track trail to our adjacent land. We dug and he was correct. Eric Gibbons owned a construction company whose jobs often required gravel. Eric called me and asked if I would sell gravel to his company. I asked, "Do you have American money?" The answer was in the affirmative and we became his supplier. Soon we entered into an agreement and he became manager of our gravel pit.

In October 2006, our daughter Monica had an immediate need for the assistance of a builder. Though Wayne Price was engaged in a project at Insel Haus, our kids' need for a builder before the onset of winter far exceeded our needs. Wayne and his crew began to work on our kids' farm home eight miles outside of Cheboygan. Our builder and crew did not discharge their responsibilities properly and finally our then son-in-law, Scott, threw members of Wayne's crew out of the house and off the property and began a series of legal actions. Even though these legal actions were underway, we exercised, as promised, our commitment to Price to sell him lot #3, one of our parcels at Lake Thompson. Wayne faced criminal charges for stealing more than $70,000 from Scott and Monica. He was also charged with four counts of larceny. After being hired by Scott and Monica to rebuild their Munro Township home he had not completed the work. He also faced trial on charges of fraudulent use of building funds. Wayne Price was found guilty and spent eight months in jail. The court took lot #3 and gave that property to Monica and Scott. Yes, he was our builder who went to jail.

GUESTS AND STORIES
A Wonderful Combination

One of the advantages of owning a Bed and Breakfast is the opportunity to meet a wonderful variety of guests. Recently, a very attractive young woman spent several nights at Insel Haus. We learned she worked for United Airlines so I automatically assumed she was a flight attendant. We were slightly off course. This young lady was a pilot.

As guests arrive at our Bed and Breakfast, I frequently challenge them to guess the furthest location on the globe from which we've had visitors. No single guest has arrived at the correct country, Mongolia. We don't believe our advertising reaches to the Mongolian steppes but there is a connection. Fiber art. The Mongolian yurt or home has been used for thousands of years by the nomads of Central Asia and is still a common sight in many countries in the region. Yurts are felted. Felting is a fiber art. Christa was a member of the Spinners Flock in Chelsea, Michigan. A fellow member visits Mongolia each year. Even keeps a horse there. She returned to Michigan with a Mongolian friend and brought her to our Bed and Breakfast. Insel Haus has three kitchens. They play a significant role in the following story. The morning before the lady was to return to our friend's Ann Arbor home Christa served coffee with whipped cream and Baileys. This is an Irish whiskey and cream-based liqueur. The guest from far off Mongolia didn't drink coffee so she just had whipped cream and Baileys. Several days later, as the woman prepared to return to Mongolia, she was asked which of the many places she had visited in the United States was her favorite. She tried to say Bois Blanc Island but found that impossible. After several unsuccessful attempts she finally blurted out "Kitchen one, Kitchen two, Kitchen three!!!" Now that's an endorsement!

Our Bed and Breakfast has hosted guests from many parts of the world. On one occasion a group from Spain and their American host arrived at the end of the season. It was the last boat of the day. They hadn't had dinner, so we sent them to the island's restaurant and general store. Unfortunately, Hawks Landing's kitchen was closed. Our guests returned to Insel Haus with the only food they could buy. Macaroni, cheese, and white bread!

As I take guests on a tour of Insel Haus I get a variety of wonderful responses to the large and very beautiful master bedroom's private bathroom with its Jacuzzi set among the tree tops. Those responses range from "wow" to "how beautiful." This time as I opened that door for these guests from Spain, I heard an "Oooh La Lah!" That was a first!

We sat and chatted with these Europeans. They quickly picked up on Christa's accent and began to speak in the most perfect and correct High German. Christa says it was so reminiscent of her grandparent's speech it almost made her cry. Several questions later we all had the answer to this seeming anomaly. It lay in the political history of their country. These men had been boys in 1939 when Francisco Franco took over the reins of power in Spain. Because of the civil war their parents had sent them to Germany to continue their education.

Their American friend and host had also come from Spain. He was an oncologist, the first physician in Michigan to implant radium seeds in the battle against prostate cancer. On hearing this I felt compelled to reveal my personal prostate cancer history. At the time I was diagnosed the current protocol dictated that if your PSA reading reached 4.1 a biopsy would be ordered. My biopsy was performed. It indicated prostate cancer. Christa and I researched the various treatment options and possible outcomes of each. We chose Watchful Waiting. And for the past 15 years I had quarterly PSA blood tests performed. My PSA readings ranged from a 2.0 to 3.0. Though we changed my diet, we did nothing medicinally. The oncologist at dinner that night said I was only one of two men he knew who had selected Watchful Waiting. He congratulated me for that decision. If you're curious about my diet this is what I chose to do. I immediately stopped eating red meat. I eat lots of chicken, turkey, fish, fruits, and vegetables. For breakfast I eat dry Cheerios, multi grain bread, give up coffee, do not drink milk, and reduce the intake of all dairy products.

One of the most unusual assignments I ever had was to produce a film honoring Mike George, leader of the Chaldean community in Detroit. All Chaldeans in Iraq come from the village of Telkaif, 30 miles from Baghdad. I believe they are the only Christians in that Moslem country. I included a scene of elderly men playing cards. They were speaking in Aramaic, a language dating back to the time of Jesus. When the lights came up after the screening a woman approached Christa. She was in tears and thanked Christa for including that card playing scene. It reminded her of her grandfather who also spoke Aramaic and died many years ago.

This experience was brought to mind yesterday when we were in a knit shop frequented by Jewish women. An elderly woman entered, sneezed and Christa said, "Gesundheit." For some inexplicable reason I immediately added, "Sultz leben a ganse yore." The woman answered, "Thank you." It was obvious she was responding emotionally. Europeans and previous generations of Jews are superstitious. What I had said in Yiddish was, "May you live a year longer as the result of that sneeze." I can't remember ever having said that before!

GUESTS AND STORIES . . .

Never. It could only have come from living with Anna, my grandmother who only spoke Yiddish and Polish. Yiddish is 14th century German. Grandma died 71 years ago when I was 14. Christa and I visited the cemetery where I believed she was buried. Amazing! With no directions or information Christa found the grave. Imbedded in the large stone marker there was my grandmother's photograph. Of course, I wept.

We recently had two guests from Northville, quite close to our Farmington Hills home. We both shop at the same large Costco shopping center. I learned Steve is a Chaldean and of course he knows Mike George. He was surprised to learn I knew of the village of Telkaif. Once again, we destroyed the myth of six degrees of separation. No question! It's only three degrees.

Another example concerned my friend Sherwin Wine, the atheist Rabbi and leader of the Humanistic Judaism movement. It too occurred at Insel Haus. A dentist arrived as a guest. We learned that he had spent three years in Morocco while serving in the U.S. military. The next day another guest appeared. He'd been Sherwin's personal dentist. Both were shocked as I informed them Sherwin Wine had recently been killed in a traffic accident . . . in Morocco. A last note on religion. About half of the 6.3 million Jews in the United States identify themselves as secular. And me? I'm an agnostic Jew who produces Catholic films! I repeat: "Life is strange and mysterious."

Before leaving the subject of synchronicity another example occurred some 60 years after my intermediate school essay on Tibet. One of our first guests at Insel Haus had just returned from that country. He'd been working there as a Christian missionary. He and his wife wrote the following commentary regarding their stay at Insel Haus.

Dear Shelby and Christa:

My wife and I are especially grateful for the experience of visiting Insel Haus, a most extraordinary retreat. We came to rest and recuperate, and our experience was beyond our hopes and expectations. Your greeting was so warm and friendly we were at ease from the start. The wonderful furnishings were not only functional but luxurious as well. The many antiques and artifacts were an endless source of discovery as each day we discovered new exciting pieces. It is an 'antique heaven' with everything tastefully done.

The last evening as a special treat we were joined by an unexpected dining guest, just outside the large windows of the Great Room. While we ate our delicious fare prepared by your culinarily artistic wife in the beautifully equipped kitchen, a doe dined on some tantalizing growth she discovered just outside the window. We also enjoyed seeing and photographing a wide variety of birds, butterflies, and other wildlife.

The accommodations provide a comfortable environment in which relaxation or group functions/seminars can take place. The key word would be "rejuvenation" for a group wishing to relax, regroup, and recharge for a new effort. I highly recommend Insel Haus as a retreat in an elegant setting where multiple objectives can be accomplished.

Thank you, Shelby and Christa, for providing such a wonderful place and for the gracious hospitality. We look forward to the next opportunity we have to get away and visit Insel Haus again.

Sincerely,
Wayne L. Brillhart

Insel Haus B&B is successful because Christa and I are committed to service. For example, the food we serve. Among our breads is Stone House. Why? Because strangely enough we believe once you know the story behind this great bread its already marvelous taste will be further enhanced.

At the big bend of Leelanau County's Eagle Highway, in a grove of century old maples, stands a small stone house as old as the trees. Otto LaBonte's daughter trudged out there every morning to turn the cream separator and to this day she calls it the Creamery. The windows and door were gone when we first saw the house, the roof leaked, and huge bumblebees cruised in to visit ancestral nests in the thick walls. We tuck-pointed the stone and fixed the roof and windows, and the building was ready now for another hundred years. Stone House Bread takes inspiration from the solid honesty of its split stone, the simple, strong lines of its architecture, and its promise certain of sturdy shelter. Our promise is the freshest bread in the North, made every morning with the finest organic flour. Fragrant crusty loaves with the sweet tang of sourdough. The baguettes and boules that emerge from our venerable Matador oven (built in Stuttgart when John Kennedy was president) will prompt memories of morning walks in Paris and Rome. We believe you'll say, with celebration: "Now that's an honest loaf of bread!"

Robert L. Pisor, Bread maker

This is sourdough bread. Yes, the power of words will affect your taste.

Insel Haus Marketing Department. Teddy Bear and "Shel" getting ready to work.

And then there is our Insel Haus Marketing Manager. Let me re-introduce Teddy Bear. To most folks he appears to be a dog. Not so! Those who know Teddy recognize he's most unusual and undoubtedly the single most valuable feature we have that induces guests to return. We mail letters and forward email advising recipients of events and activities occurring on Bois Blanc or at our B&B. They all carry his title, Marketing Manager.

Here's an example:

This may be the first letter you've received from a dog, but don't let that throw you. I can handle English. After all, it's my second language. I'm a mixture of Collie, Akita, and Malamute. Shelby determined I'm mostly Malamute because I enjoy lying down in the snow and falling asleep. I remember your arrival at Insel Haus. Shel, I call him that, introduced us and in his typical straight-faced manner said I was dangerous. Might kiss you to death! He meant well, but that was a slight exaggeration. I'll be 13 in March, so I've been studying people for a long time. Your body language was loud and clear. You needed rest and you sure came to the right place. I can attest to that since I rest most of the time. I'm convinced you had a great visit.

But, as a Collie I used to hang out with would say, "You ain't seen nothin' yet!" Winter at Insel Haus is fantastic! Check out the pristine beauty that surrounds us. I don't mean to wax poetic, but as a pup in the city I never knew snow was white until I was brought to Bois Blanc Island. Can't wait to see this year's blanket of snow on the evergreens surrounding the meadow. The overhead power line has been buried. Thought I knew how to dig! Those guys were pros. Remember how the tree line used to be great? Now it's spectacular! Wonder if Shelby will feed the deer again this winter? Last year they had a ball. He got them drunk on molasses and corn. Ever seen deer dancing? Personally, I don't see what's so hot about cross-country skiing or snowshoes, but our guests think they're terrific. Must be a people thing. Come to Insel Haus this winter. I promise to show you around. Winter, summer, spring or fall, Christa, Shelby, and I want to share it all with you.

Teddy Bear
Marketing Manager
Insel Haus B&B

Here is one of the many responses Teddy Bear received.

Sept. 20, 2006

Teddy Bear
Marketing Manager
Insel Haus

Hi Teddy Bear,

    It was great to see you looking so handsome and fit. I know you were glad to see us by the sparkle in your eye. We all had lots of fun with your other guests. It was a great time. The food was delicious thanks to Christa. The new addition to Insel Haus is awesome. Christa has great ideas and gets them done. I'll be anxious to hear about the wedding held in the outdoor room. I'm sure it was beautiful. Joan is having knee trouble so she is off to the doctor. If the knee is O.K. we plan to see you. Will let you know.

Love to all.

Assistant Marketing Manager,
Grace

    Teddy developed a relationship with the deer herd on our property. Deer are not stupid. They learned he wouldn't chase them. He'd just lie down and study them. Make sure they'd be safe.

Teddy relaxing under the oaks. Looking wise and totally in charge.

Sadly, Teddy left us at the age of 13. What a loss. Many guests commiserated with us. Christa posted the following on our web site.

Nov. 24, 2008

The wet snow covers last night's footprints, even the ones made on the Cairns for Oma and Opa. The indentation in the high grass of the meadow, made when there was the need for a moment of peaceful rest, is still visible. Did you hear the deer in the forest? Thirty-two wild turkeys create 10-lane highways, with their footprints erasing yours, but never the memory of you. Dearest Teddy, thank you for all your love. Keep looking into the windows of our souls. And today we will burn our tears.

FRIENDS!

In the spring of 2008 Kristi Burr read the Land for Sale notice on the Insel Haus web site. She and husband Jeff came from their home in Burton, Ohio and Christa took them for a walk of our property. They indicated an interest in land, but not individual parcels. It was important to them that the property remain intact. I'm convinced their interest was heightened by the timely call of a Sandhill Crane. This beautiful creature had become a member of our negotiating team. The discussion continued while they took us to lunch at the Bob-Lo Tavern. We learned Kristi was a medical advocate and executive director of a foundation committed to assisting victims of a particular form of skin cancer, the Gorlin syndrome. Jeff was a successful farmer as well as a maple syrup manufacturer and distributor.

On May 30, Kristi and her retired lawyer friend, 84-year-old Bill Ginn, attended a land conservancy meeting held on nearby Mackinac Island. They took advantage of the opportunity to visit Bois Blanc. They evidenced an interest in Insel Haus and our future plans. Christa remembered an experience with a very wise carpenter. As he unrolled his tape measure, he asked Christa to imagine each inch to be one year. Then he asked her to imagine how long she might live. Christa noted the long distance she'd already lived and the short distance remaining. The carpenter's point was well taken. It was time to seriously consider how we'd spend our remaining years. Yes, Insel Haus would be available for purchase.

Kristi and her Foundation appeared to be likely purchasers. We drove to Burton, Ohio and were guests of her attorney, Bill Ginn. This was the first of a series of meetings, involved negotiations, and the raising of our hopes over a period of many months. Sadly, the deal fell through. But our good relationship continues to this day. Kristi Burr, the Executive Director of the BCCNS Foundation scheduled the first of three retreats at Insel Haus. When Larry Phillips, owner of Hawks Landing, our island's combined general store and restaurant, learned the group would include a number of children he went into action, demonstrating what a thoughtful, kind, generous person he is. He bought fishing poles and tackle boxes for each youngster. The kids went fishing. Of course, it was catch and release. A 10-year-old girl caught 25 fish and won their contest. The highlight of the retreat was an event I'd never seen before. A butterfly release! Kristi Burr ordered a box of butterflies. The package was mailed to Insel Haus. In the early afternoon, when the sun is nice and warm and the sweet smell of milkweed fills the air, the release takes place. Each child and adult is given a small envelope. The envelope is warmed by holding it between your hands. You close your eyes, make a wish . . . then slowly open the small envelope to watch the monarch begin to awaken, move, open its wings, and fly.

Our friends DeLaine and Chip took the kids to the beach and collected rocks. These were brought back to our deck where the kids had great fun painting them. Then DeLaine took a flat rock about a foot long and painted the words "PLEASE TURN ME OVER!" The kids did just that and found what she'd written on the other side. "AHHHH! THAT FEELS BETTER." The kids found it. The kids got it. The kids turned it over. The kids loved it. This kid wished he could claim authorship.

April 28, 2009. A rather important event occurred today. It coincided with the arrival of the first ferry following the winter season. During the winter the Straits freeze so we arrive and depart from Bois Blanc by plane. Today's ferry had no passengers. Instead, the boat had a cargo of propane gas trucks. They were being brought across to fill homeowners' gas tanks. Insel Haus has four of these tanks. I was at my computer doing research. Not feeling very well, I decided to take a break. I lay down and slept for half an hour. On awakening, I experienced difficulty attempting to form words. Christa called Plaunt's Ferry and told Lee she had to get me to a hospital at once. Lee called back quickly saying that Ryan, the young captain, would come to Insel Haus and help get me to the boat.

Ryan helped me move into Christa's car. We drove the mile to the dock and boarded the Kristen D. Carrying a passenger requires a deck hand as well as the captain. Ryan was the only sailor on the ferry, so Larry Phillips raced to the boat and jumped aboard to act as the necessary deck hand.

Christa asked both Ryan and Larry to which hospital would they take a member of their family if they were ill? The immediate response was the Northern Michigan Hospital at Petoskey. Forty-five minutes later we drove off the ferry at the Cheboygan dock and took off for the hour drive to Petoskey. As we arrived at the emergency entrance I felt nauseous, opened the car door, and threw up on the pavement. Christa got a wheelchair and pushed me to the admitting desk. When she returned after parking her car they asked my first name. I apparently was able to say Newhouse, but unable to pronounce my first name, Shelby.

I was admitted immediately, tests were run, but I had already passed beyond the three-hour window during which attempts to treat a stroke are possible. They took me to a room with a beautiful view of the Straits of Mackinac and were prepared to place me in a bed when they discovered this patient whose name was Shelby was a male! The patient in the next bed was a woman. "I said I don't mind." Her daughter said, "No way! My mother might mind." I was moved to another room.

Our daughter Monica arrived. She and Christa spent the night at the hospital's hospitality house. My son Dana arrived the next day. My daughter, Erin, who lived in Austin, Texas arrived the following day. I continued to have many tests including an MRI. What they discovered was that I had experienced the ultimate stroke of luck.

The neurological surgeon sat on the edge of my bed and made a truly remarkable statement. What he had to say could only be based on his interpretation of my medical condition. He wasn't passing judgment on my character or me as a person. We had never met. He had no reason to be angry or upset with me. It was obvious his only concern was my medical condition. These were his exact words. "You should be dead"! Christa had been standing for many hours. She was so shocked she sat down on the porta-potty. Here was a classic example of our physician's bedside manner. Every doctor should memorize that phrase. You should be dead! How better to demonstrate your sympathy for your patient's illness?

I wanted a further explanation of my condition. I asked for a drawing of what had taken place. "No time," he said. "Have to see other patients. Your condition is inoperable. I will do a world-wide search to see if anyone has been able to operate." And he walked out, just left. How's that for bedside manner? According to the textbooks he was correct. What the x-rays and other tests showed was that I had a congenital condition affecting the two basal arteries that supply blood to the brain. Since birth they'd always been too small and narrow to do their job as intended. Over the past 82 years other adjacent vessels had been helping supply the required blood. On April 28, 2009, I had experienced a blood clot that resulted in the complete shutdown of these basal arteries. This in fact was an inoperable condition. But the corollary vessels had taken over and were now doing the entire job for which the basal arteries were intended. A great example of patient heal thyself. At 82, the ultimate stroke of luck!

This same day while in the hospital Christa received a call from American Express. They were asking about a bill that was due. The representative recognized Christa's accent and continued the conversation in German. When she described the present circumstances, he said don't worry about that bill. We'll take care of it. Handle it when you can. His compassion in contrast to the surgeon's was striking.

May 8, 2009

Dear Harriet,

Now that I've recovered from my "Stroke of Luck" let me tell you how very much I appreciate your love and concern. This has been a truly unique experience since my last hospitalization was Nov. 22, 1926, (my birth). The staff and doctors at Northern Michigan Hospital were marvelous. At no time was there any pain associated with my condition.

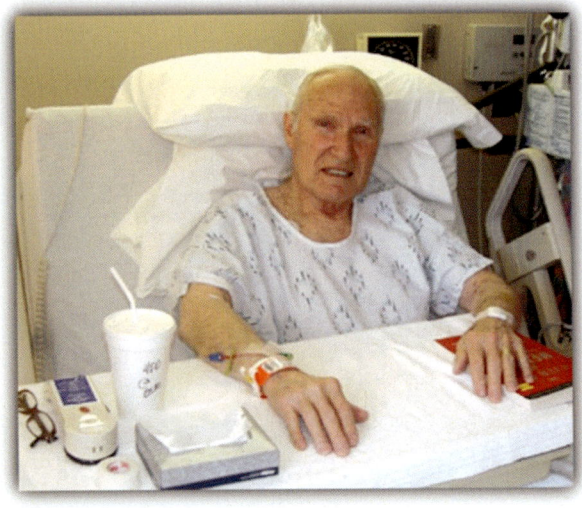

Thus far the only pain has been economic. I have been advised I am now a contributor to the pharmaceutical industry. I offered an annual contribution, but they insist it be daily. In truth, I feel excellent. Lucky to have had this wakeup call and I promise to continue my habit of no smoking, no alcohol, and no coffee.

           Love,
           Shelby

So, I'd had a stroke. But could talk, walk, and even run! The only measurable result? My memory has been affected. One positive consequence, my 3,000-book personal library, books on a bewildering array of subjects, truly eclectic, was now new.

Two radio men just hanging out. Talking awards and books with my multi-talented friend John Robinson, longtime host on 99.1 WFMK East Lansing, Michigan.

I confess, the one I enjoy the most is Alan King's "Great Jewish Joke Book." Example: Moishe, a tailor, and God were discussing going into business together. Seeking a good name both agreed "Moishe and God" wouldn't work. Then God came up with a dilly! "Lord and Taylor."

On Aug. 5, 2012, Christa's 72nd birthday, she had a request. Would I please read aloud Mark Twain's story of Tom Sawyer and Huckleberry Finn? In the section of my library devoted to the classics I found "The Adventures of Huckleberry Finn." The very first page indicates why Christa loves Twain's sense of humor. It reads:

> NOTICE: Persons attempting to find a motive in this narrative will be prosecuted; persons attempting to find a moral in it will be banished; persons attempting to find a plot in it will be shot. By Order Of The Author Per G, G, Chief of Ordinance.

As always, I deferred to my wonderful wife's request. I read Mark Twain . . . aloud.

On a related subject: libraries. In the winter we live in a truly wonderful town. I've been going to libraries all my life, but I've never seen a more successful asset to a community than our Farmington Hills, Michigan library. Though I'm not aware of any survey on the subject I'm convinced there are more children than adults using our library. In addition to the many computers available and meeting rooms used for a variety of programs there are racks of DVDs from the U.S. and many foreign countries. Approaching the parking area yesterday I saw what would have made a wonderful commercial. Three children, probably ages 5, 7 and 9, pulling their mother to get into the library!

Yes. Our local library is wonderful. But the other day I witnessed a sad event. While older siblings were selecting their books, a small boy, probably 3 years old, had been given a magazine to occupy and entertain him. He was obviously getting extremely frustrated and was about to cry. No matter how much he tried moving his hands and fingers on that colorful picture on the cover, that picture would not move, change, or grow smaller or larger. Talk about advancing technology and change. I realize this poor child will grow up never having had the opportunity of entering a street-corner telephone booth or placing his hand on the telephone and turning the dial! Perhaps the most constant element in life is change. There will be change. Not only in the weather, but virtually everything. Count on it.

Though I can no longer remember many past events, when activities surrounding the event are described I often do recall them. An example occurred the other day. Christa and I were visiting the genius bar, an Apple computer shop at the local mall. A fellow approached us calling out, "Shelby Newhouse and Christa Kindt!"

He extended his hand asking, "Remember me? I'm Sheldon Nueman."

"I know your name," I said. "But I've had a stroke and don't recall how we know each other."

"Shelby, you took me to Portugal"!

"Wow!" I replied. "You were my soundman. Shel Nueman"!

It all came back to me. The scene outside the farmhouse, the farmer's goats, Shel lying on the ground on the goat's output, holding his microphone as we shot that wonderful interview with the elderly farmer and his wife telling of their being a witness to the miracle of Fatima. We stood in the Apple computer store and had a great chat during which he noted his career had advanced rapidly after working with me. All he had to tell other producers was that he had been on shoots with Shelby Newhouse. What a great compliment!

There may be something metaphysical involved in the following. Who knows? Last night I dreamt about Phyllis' father, my first father-in-law, Herbert McCreedy and the men around him. Today, as I walked along the parking area of our dock, I couldn't help but notice a car covered head to stern with slogans supporting President Obama, Israel, Gay Pride, and a host of other liberal causes. I was compelled to knock on the driver's window. He called me Shelby, knew of Insel Haus and remembered me from my radio-TV days. In our conversation I learned he had known Herb McCreedy, Gus Scholle, Tom Downs, and other democrats from the 1940s. When I produced the Diego Rivera documentary Tom Downs' daughter Linda was the DIA's Curator of Education. We were a team in the making of the story of Rivera's frescoes, "The Age of Steel." This new friend and I planned to meet soon at Insel Haus and continue our conversation.

As I write this chapter, I know Erin and her minister husband, Tom, are praying for me. My nephew, Gary Glickstein, a Rabbi with a temple and congregation in Miami is also praying for me. Here at the Coast Guard Chapel on Bois Blanc Island the Baptist minister also asked the congregation to pray for Shelby Newhouse. "He is Jewish"! Friends of mine seated in the chapel were offended. I pointed out that this minister was only seeking to improve my condition. He was thinking of my well-being and encouraging me to come to Christ. It appears this agnostic Jew is covered. Can't ask for more than that.

CHANGE, THE ONLY CONSTANT

About 2010 the convergence of events resulted in Christa taking unprecedented actions. The film business had changed drastically. There were fewer opportunities for editing assignments. Unique Film & Video was suffering. My advanced age of 84 resulted in my being out of the loop. I was no longer networking, seeking opportunities for producing, writing, or directing films. The drastic slide in the U.S. economy meant the average American's discretionary dollars had disappeared. One of the results was a reduction in bookings at Insel Haus. Mortgage payments for our Bois Blanc business continued to be almost $5,000 a month.

We had sold the Annex building. Christa moved her editing equipment to our Cass home and continued editing there. I was at the B&B taking care of our guests when Christa took her father's gold wedding ring and several of her own pieces of jewelry and sold them. She carried several of our Persian rugs to Hagopian, the most famous rug merchant in Michigan. She was offering them for sale but refused to discuss them with any of the salespersons. Christa insisted on showing the rugs to Mrs. Hagopian. The owner of the company told her they were valuable, but due to the terrible economy she'd be wise to hold on to them until the economy improved.

It did for us. More strokes of luck!

Thank you, Beth Beson! When you entered our lives perhaps a dozen years ago it would have been impossible to foresee the role you would ultimately play. We called you our 'angel'. As new Bed and Breakfast entrepreneurs, every piece of income was important. You purchased our gift certificates, which you then donated to various charitable organizations that in turn sold them to raise funds for their church or organization.

We have since learned who you are, what you are, and how you have assumed a major role in our lives. The definition of a philanthropist is someone who makes charitable donations intended to increase human well-being. Christa and I qualify as human beings and our well-being has immeasurably increased as a result of your actions. Permit us to present a partial list:

Prepping for a BCCNS event, Instant Inn Keeper, Window washer, Sign painter, On-time banker, Misty Pines advisor, Weed whacker, Hammock provider, Safe cracker, Flower planter, Repairer of vacuum cleaners, Cleaner of bathrooms, Bat researcher, Making Christa's doctor visits possible, Purchaser of our Bois Blanc Island land, all around friend!!!! Undoubtedly, I've missed any number of other examples of how you've improved our lives. Thank you,

Beth. We speak not only for ourselves, but the countless other recipients of your goodwill and assistance who often remain unaware of their benefactor. Your purchase of 150 acres of our island land made it possible for us to retire the mortgage on Insel Haus! Yes! We now owned our home, Insel Haus, FREE and CLEAR! Our mortgage had been retired!

Beth also bought Monica and Scott's Lake Thompson lot #3. This transaction made it possible for our kids to recover some of their losses.

Beth, we love you!

Our dear friend Sheila was spending a week with us at Insel Haus a few days in advance of her 75th birthday. Something was troubling her. Timeshare points were going to be lost since she couldn't use them before the end of the year. Christa immediately recognized a solution and asked, "Could we help?" We had been contemplating a trip to California to visit Harriet, my 86-year-old sister, who was recovering from open-heart surgery. To pay for hotels and meals on the road presented a serious problem. This might be the answer. If we could stay at timesharing locations, we'd be able to visit Harriet in Calabasas, visit my son Kim in Long Beach, and Christa's brother Klaus in San Diego. Our good friend made the necessary phone calls and we were booked at the Oasis in Palm Springs! It was a double header! Both problems were solved!

We departed from our Cass house at 10 a.m. the day before Thanksgiving, Wednesday, Nov. 24, 2010. This was to be the longest extended trip we had ever undertaken in our 29 years of marriage. Though Christa permits me to drive on the island, I was destined to become a passenger on the mainland. Christa drove over 5,000 miles and it took five weeks! We spent the first night in the Clarion Inn of little Amana, Iowa. As we were ready to leave for dinner Christa pointed out my shirt was not in my pants, the pants were not zipped up, and the belt wasn't buckled. It appeared I was ready for anything! On reflection I suspect my actions were an indication of my advanced age! Dinner was at Grandma's Kitchen. Unfortunately, Grandpa was cooking.

We were in for a great surprise the next morning. As we drove west on I-90 our car lost power. That's a unique feeling. Seventy miles an hour and suddenly coasting to a stop at the side of the highway! But guess what? An Iowa Highway Patrol officer's car was sitting right there! Now, that's a once-in-a-lifetime event. We could have traveled hundreds of miles and never seen a traffic cop. Officer Jon Degen was great! He said, "It's 22 degrees. You'll freeze sitting in your car waiting for help. Get in, you're coming with me." This was Thanksgiving morning. I noted that I'd never before heard a police officer say, "You're coming with me!" Nor had I experienced the pleasure of sitting in a patrol car. He called a tow truck, drove us to a small-town diner and as he left Officer Degen said, "Wait here and look for a driver in a red shirt." Never knew red shirts were so popular in Iowa. One of the many nice guys wearing red shirts that were dropping in for coffee offered to drive us wherever we needed to go. "After all," he said, "its Thanksgiving. Oh! California? Sorry. Out of my way."

Two hours later the real thing arrived, BJ of BJ's Towing. He drove us to our dead car, hauled it onto his truck, and took off for the nearest inn where we could spend the night. Making small talk he mentioned he had experienced nine, count them, nine strokes in the last five years. I took this opportunity to mention my stroke two years earlier at the age of 82. How lucky I was. I could talk, walk, and even run. But my memory had been affected. It was the only deficit as a result of that stroke. I said there are many things I can't remember. And this lady sitting next to me claims to be my wife! I bet he took that story home! In truth, he was a smarty-cat. His diagnosis of our problem turned out to be correct. It was the fuel pump and he'd have to travel to Iowa City the next day to get one.

Dinner and breakfast at the inn were not advertisements for Iowa. Before checking out we experienced two meals. The waitress for each was unique. Either girl could have been anywhere in the world, but certainly not at our table. Their efforts to take our orders left me with a true sense of compassion for the inn's owner. Desert was accompanied by what Christa claimed was perfume. Only a master chef could determine if it had been poured on the girl or the food.

The next day, 12:10 p.m. Central Time, our car finally arrived, driven by a mechanic with no name or personality. He drove us to BJ's. Unbelievable! It looked like a movie set. Dilapidated, run down, unhappy dog tethered to a chain. And guess what? They'd never heard of checks or credit cards. That's right! It had to be cash on the barrelhead, and they had the barrel! Christa shelled out $954.54 to retrieve our vehicle. The rest of the trip with only $50 in cash wasn't half bad!

Each day we spoke with Harriet. She was still confined to her hospital bed, but it was wonderful to note her continued improvement. As we drove off the next morning we were delighted to see flocks of geese above us. They numbered in the thousands and like us, they were engaged on their journey.

After we left the Comfort Inn in Kearney, Nebraska Christa took us to Loveland, Colorado in an effort to visit the Interweave Press. As a knitter and knitting teacher she had looked forward to this visit. They were closed, but the city was an art center with many sculptures. We were in the foothills of the Rocky Mountains on a road traveled by Greyhound bus lines. Here were towns named by prospectors and folks opening the western frontiers. They had out-of-this-world monikers. No Name was only 1/2 mile from No Where!

Our stay at the Comfort Inn in Grand Junction, Colorado prepared us for entry into Utah and sensational vistas. The price of gas in Thompson, Utah was also sensational, $3.29 per gallon!!! At the summit of 7,800 feet a road sign read "Watch Out for Deer and Elk on Road." It began to snow. Plows were on the road, our wipers worked constantly, and our hazard blinkers were on! With limited visibility we drove by the Kanab Road exit #98 and a sign advertising a dealer in Indian Antiques. Did that ever bring back memories! Years before, my daughter Erin and I had taken a wonderful trip and had met an antique dealer in Kanab. We were invited to his home where he planned to show us many Indian artifacts.

Father-daughter trip with a stop in Kanab, Utah.

After entering his lovely adobe home, we discovered an original painting behind the door. It was the work of Diego Rivera. As exciting as this discovery was, Erin's response to our trip was something I truly treasure. In her words, "It was the best trip and adventure I'd ever had with my dad."

Our next view was scary and dangerous. It was a truck pulling a large house trailer. It could only be described as slipping and sliding! Dangerous! I thought if a driver needed a rest stop this would not be the place. The safest thing to do was to stay on I-15 for the next 212 miles! The following day we were relieved to see that truck driver and his house trailer again. He made it!

The next summit was at 5,900 feet. Las Vegas, Nevada was only 157 miles dead ahead. We drove past many cars that had slid off the highway. Though the speed limit read 70 mph our speed was about 35! In fact, as we reached the next summit with an elevation of 5,000 feet, we faced an actual whiteout. We dropped down to 3,000 feet at Green Springs, Utah. Now we were only 109 miles from the gambling capital of the world, Las Vegas! It seemed logical to have dinner in a casino. We were under the mistaken illusion their food would be good and the price reasonable! Surprise! Not true. We also learned smoking is permitted in both the gambling hall and their restaurant.

My driver now recognized my advanced age. So every time our gas gauge read half a tank we pulled over to a gas station. Christa could fill the Suburban's tank. I could empty mine!

On Nov. 28 we arrived at a beautiful condo in Palm Springs. Thank you, Sheila! Here were two bedrooms though we only used one, a full kitchen, washing machine, dryer, and two bicycles in the garage. Wow! Palm Springs, all it's cracked up to be!

Now, I had to pay attention to business. This meant a blood test to check the level of my warfarin. We drove to a hospital and learned they no longer accepted out-of-state prescriptions. We were directed to a clinic and the blood was drawn. The results were relayed to Cathy, my nurse practitioner in St. Ignace. Her office called us. I was told to maintain my regular regimen and have the test taken again in two weeks. Now we could behave like vacationers and tourists. We shopped for food and washing detergent and then visited the Living Desert display where we bought food for birds at our home in Farmington Hills.

It was now Nov. 30. By calling my niece Hillary, we learned Harriet would undergo a lung procedure the next day and then be released. Two days later, Dec. 2, we headed for Calabasas and Harriet. It was a 2 1/2-hour drive.

California . . . what a unique experience. Found my sister very weak, very slender, but as always, a gracious hostess. She sent Anna, her live-in nurse assistant, for bagels, lox, and cream cheese. Harriet's spirits were good but since we chose not to tire her, we made it a short visit and left for Palm Springs with the promise to return soon.

The trip back to the condo can only be described as a nightmare. It wasn't just that the drive took more than five hours. The environment and attitudes of our fellow travelers had to be experienced to be believed. At one point we sat behind the same truck for an hour! I tried to remember the name of my worst enemy to wish this ride upon him, but I failed. Absolutely no one who had earned this came to mind.

Dec. 2, we attempted to schedule a service call at the local Chevrolet dealership but were told it would have to be done the next day. Rather than wait we visited a local mechanic at an oil changing station. Paul was both good and accommodating. After our car was inspected, he called to inform us there was a leak in the power steering system which could be repaired by the next day. That night he called to describe the 2 1/2 hours he'd spent getting a bolt off the vehicle. He had no previous experience with Michigan rust. Our car was scheduled to be delivered at 9:30 the following morning. Christa's brother Klaus arrived from San Diego. It was wonderful! The day turned out to be one of the highlights of our vacation. He spent the night and left in the morning.

Before departing on our journey, friends of ours had insisted we enjoy the "Fabulous Follies" in Palm Springs. Christa made the connections and purchased two front-row seats for the Dec. 3 performance. This burlesque show was everything we'd been promised. Ziegfeld's it wasn't. But even he would have enjoyed it. The emcee was a Yiddish comedian. I believe the youngest of the dancers was in her late 60s, the oldest 86! Bodies still worth looking at, perhaps even studying, their dancing was very professional and the costumes worthy of off-Broadway. Even though you may have heard some of the jokes before, the timing was great! The audience was with them all the way! We really enjoyed the show. I'd recommend it to anyone over 15.

Dec. 4 was a great day! Just relaxing. We spent time at the World Market followed by a short visit to Estate Sales stores. Christa loved a rosewood table and chairs and two special chairs with footrests, but she was strong. We didn't buy anything.

Dec. 5 included two visits. The first was to Harriet, who clearly was on the road to recovery. This was also an opportunity to meet Dixon, her Pomeranian dog. What a great companion.

A visit in California at an earlier time.

My wonderful sister Harriet. Always the great collector.

The second was a visit with my son Kim in Long Beach. He insisted on taking us to lunch. We ate at an outdoor café. This gave us an opportunity to observe the community while discussing life in Long Beach and his work at Home Depot. He continues to write screenplays and deliver them to his Hollywood contacts. What a tough game. Kim is a far better writer than I will ever be, but you have to have luck and opportunities. Love him! Wish he were closer to our home.

VISTAS, COLOR, AND FIBER

A cedar chest in our Insel Haus Great Room has been painted to tell Christa's story. Alpacas are shown along with this text:

A Yarn Dreamer's Tale

I have been captured by Alpacas.

My journey began 70 years ago in Berlin, Germany. I entered the United States as a motion picture editor in 1964. After 43 years in film, and a life with a menagerie that included 12 cats, five dogs, 9 geese, several chickens, and Jimmy the Rooster, I met Honeycomb the Alpaca. Then the past became prologue. Her fabulous eyes, gentle nature, incredibly soft fleece, and humming sounds introduced a new phase in my life. I fell in love with this gift from the Andes, and now I have Star of Bethlehem, Queen of Sheba, Alhambra del Fuego, Rhett Butler, and Tahitian Pearl providing fleece to create one-of-a-kind hand-spun yarns and garments for you to treasure and enjoy!!

Our alpaca herd grew with each cria until we had 11. They were never kept on Bois Blanc Island. They were living on alpaca farms where others cared for them, bred them, attended to all their needs. The term is egested. We harvested their fleece, which Christa spun and sold to other knitters.

In 2011 we sold our last alpaca. This was the closing of another chapter in our wonderful adventure and the beginning of Christa's journey into a world of teaching and designing knitted garments under the name of Yarn Dreamer.

Christa showing Rhett Butler at the longest-running Alpaca show in the United States.

From start to finish.

Spinning on the Island.

A knitting and spinning retreat at Insel Haus.

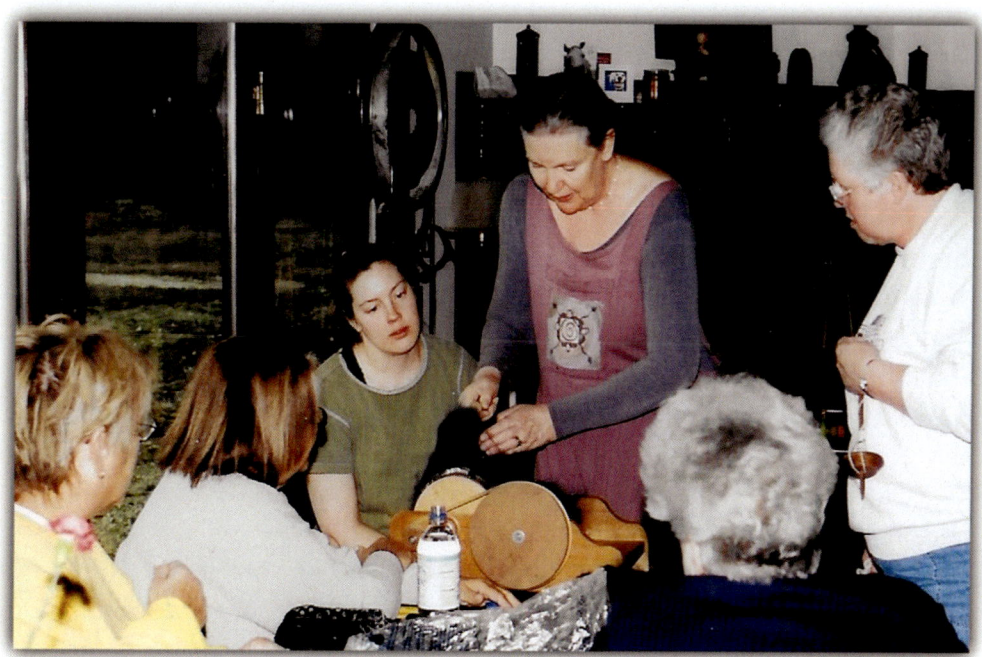

Another Insel Haus retreat. Christa demonstrating how to use the drum carder.

Yarn Dreamer. As a fiber artist, Christa's use of color is a very important component of her work. We were now on the road to Santa Fe, New Mexico, to spend a week in another timeshare donated by Sheila. Our journey had special significance for Christa. Color! The vistas and even the architecture introduced a powerful use of strong basic colors. Looking at garments Christa has produced since that trip demonstrates how important that experience was.

As always, whenever we are on the road, knit shops present the strongest attraction. Soon a shop owner noticed Christa's German accent and asked if she knew Valentina Divine, a fellow Berliner and knitting teacher. We drove to Taos in the mountains to meet Valentina. In her home studio we saw an unbelievable collection of hand-dyed yarns and textures. We learned she teaches throughout the United States including Lexington, Michigan. We were also introduced to her husband, a nuclear scientist. He was among those who had worked at Los Alamos, the federal government's secret laboratory in north central New Mexico. There is no way to properly place a value on such chance encounters. Meeting interesting people, learning, and observing.

Visiting antique stores included the purchase of a beautiful rug for our friend and benefactor, Beth Beson.

On one of our visits to a gallery Christa experienced shortness of breath. This was not a reaction to the beauty of the pieces of art on display. It wasn't this that took her breath away. It was the altitude. The nice saleslady directed us to the center of town where there was an oxygen bar that was there precisely for this purpose. She explained this condition was not unusual. The adjustment to the new altitude usually took two days. Christa discovered she didn't need that bar. And on reflection was reminded how significant it was that she had stopped smoking in 1972.

We noticed a local movie house was playing the new film, "Burlesque." This film's casting of today's young, vibrant, exciting performers was a fascinating contrast to what we had experienced at the Follies in Palm Springs. Our trip to New Mexico also included an opportunity to visit Jennifer Barclay's Blue Fish store in Taos. Since 1995 Christa had been addicted to wearing this line of women's clothing. She disciplined herself. We didn't spend a dime there!

Our next stop was Austin, Texas. The next few days were spent in our usual bedroom in our daughter Tania and Trace's house. Coco, their cat immediately disappeared under their bed never to be seen again during our stay. But we were treated to the regular feeding session of outdoor cats. Our activities included great meals, a trip to their church, and visit to my daughter Erin and her husband Tom's RV Park. They had both retired, sold their house and belongings, and bought a fifth-wheel trailer and diesel truck. They were ready to travel the universe!

Tom took us to a roller-skating rink to see our great-grandchildren Persephone and Leila in action. Persephone won every contest competing against all comers! Yes, we were proud! Our trip to Austin ended with a great dinner get-together. My great-grandson Jonathan had brought my granddaughter Rebecca and her husband Bob from Houston. Persephone brought Leila, Josh, Erin and Tom and we brought Tania and Trace to our favorite Chinese restaurant. We posed for a family portrait of all of us crowding around PF Chang's huge horses at the entrance of this restaurant.

On our continuing return trip to Michigan, we made several stops. First to visit DeLaine and Warren in Texas, friends from Bois Blanc Island. We arrived out of the blue asking, "What's for lunch?" What a surprise for them! We also visited Sharon and Dave Spaulding in Shreveport, Louisiana. Dave was the radiologist who had explained the function of the Circle of Willis to Christa while I was recovering from my stroke. Both he and Sharon had taken over the running of Insel Haus for a day or two while I was in the hospital.

The next stop was an exploratory trip to the John C. Campbell Folk School in Brasstown, North Carolina. Christa had been invited to teach knitting at this folk school. I thought that was strange since every school teaches folks! It didn't take long for her to straighten me out. The John C. Campbell Folk School did not teach readin', writin', an 'rithmetic! It had been founded in 1925 as a unique institution to bring out the best in people through performing arts, agriculture, and crafts rooted in the traditions of Southern Appalachia and other cultures in the world. Kisha, the assistant program director, a warm, friendly, marvelous representative of both the school and surrounding rural area introduced us to the school. Since we were both senior citizens, she asked us about our past. What kind of work we'd been doing. I answered we were filmmakers. And since she was a beautiful African American, I mentioned our film, "Heritage in Black." Kisha gasped, "I've seen your film. Let me give you a hug!" Now, that's the best kind of film appreciation I've ever received.

The next stop was Ohio to visit Kristi and Bill. They took us to dinner, made arrangements for us to stay in a B&B in Burton, Ohio. All expenses paid! Our purpose was to arrange for the next BCCNS retreat at Insel Haus. A date was set and we continued on our way. We returned hugging the shoreline of Lake Erie. Christa had become a Michigander. She missed the Great Lakes.

Two months passed and it was time to head out from Insel Haus to drive to Brasstown, North Carolina. Our arrival was on Feb. 20, 2011. The school must have a lock on the weather. There was snow on our island when we left, but here in Appalachia there were daffodils peeking their heads out of the ground. Christa's classroom offers everything she and her students would ever need in pursuit of the art of knitting in this non-competitive environment. Housing?

Appropriately enough our room with private bath was in the Farm House. I pen this after the first three days at this folk school. If eating is no more than an exercise required by your body to function, it may be because you've never experienced meals at the John C. Campbell Folk School. I rest my fork!

And by the way, don't let anyone tell you there's no nightlife in this part of the world. Last evening an interesting, friendly, dulcimer and guitar-playing teacher invited us to a community band concert in nearby Young Harris, Georgia, a college town. What a concert! An indication of the quality of these musicians is their upcoming European tour. The concert band will play in Prague, Munich, and Vienna.

To adequately comment on the Folk School experience would be to simply prepare a lengthy list of superlatives. First the students! Every single one was prepared and eager to learn. At the end of the week they were no longer students, but friends. The facility was perfect, food wonderful, lodging all we could have desired. My vocabulary fails me as I try to capture the atmosphere. Warm, friendly, congenial, welcoming . . . down home! We look forward to more Campbell Folk School teaching opportunities in the future.

What was it like in North Carolina? First of all, we were in the mountains. Christa relived her past. It was as if she were back in the Alps. The roads were in great shape and challenging to drive since it was curve after curve after curve. There were hardly any sections that were straight. The views were wonderful. As a passenger on the hills of this state I was in a constant state of WOW!

There's no question the Campbell Folk School is in America, but I'm not sure if it is really on a map. Folks are friendly and eager to engage you in conversation and communication was no problem. Their accent was lovely. There was only one exception at a small restaurant. The waitress and I did have a problem. I was at a total loss to understand anything she said. Fortunately, I could read the menu and point to what I chose to order.

We were invited to visit the home of Tom and Gretchen. Over 9,000-square-feet on top of the highest mountain in the area. The view was spectacular and by the way, Tom, a local dentist, was building an airplane inside the house. The fact that I've been growing a full beard played well here. Those of us with hairy faces outnumbered the clean-shaven guys 2-to-1! I really fit in. And two subjects never surfaced in any conversation: politics or religion. Though the rest of the country was experiencing a tough winter our sunups and sundowns were spectacular. As I conclude this paragraph Christa has again received another invitation to return to North Carolina and teach at the Campbell Folk School in 2013. Yes, once again I will tag along. Christa's reputation as a teacher of advanced knitting techniques had been growing. As evidence: She taught again in Lake Orion, Michigan this weekend. Tonight she received a call from a shop in Lexington, Michigan and will teach there soon. Then Minnesota. In a few days we leave for a week at a knit shop in Ames, Iowa.

Ames, Iowa! A college town, home to the University of Iowa and a large community of Norwegian expatriates. Among them, Arnhild Hillesland, a resident for many years, but not a citizen of the U.S. She vows to return to her native land when her husband Glenn dies. Arnhild's Knitting Studio was our next stop for a full weekend of teaching. Imagine! Twenty students in a class. I was to model several garments, entertain the assembled ladies, and stay out of the way. During dinner a model walked around the room displaying Christa's swing coat and matching hat. Its design was the skyline of Chicago. The moon is shown beginning to appear from behind one of the many buildings. Since this was an example of double knitting the coat could be worn revealing the inside as well. Then the moon became the sun. Assembled guests learned there were no seams and there were 3,500 stitches around the bottom of the garment. This piece had been independently appraised at thousands of dollars. The knitter's response to this extraordinary, beautiful work can be judged by the reaction of one of those present. She was a worldly-wise former 20-year member of our U.S. military. She was moved to tears. Evidence of Christa's success was the request to return again next year.

On the return trip from Ames, we once more experienced why we love to take drives in the country. It was just a stop for lunch and a walk to stretch our legs. The small town was West Branch, Iowa, the birthplace of President Herbert Hoover. It's downtown consists of one block, including a bank building with intricate carvings at each corner and the date 1906. There were two antique shops. We speculated how many days it would take to prepare an inventory of their contents. Christa loved looking through the building's old plate glass. Everything appeared to be bent. And she had never seen an old small banner attached to one door. I knew what it represented and explained the significance of the star in its center. This was probably hung during World War II. Here lived a Gold Star mother. She had lost a son in that war.

Since this was a typical midwestern town I thought I was probably the only man walking those streets sporting a ponytail. Wrong! Before leaving we had seen three men with beards and ponytails. Seeking lunch we stopped at a Mexican restaurant. The door was locked. West Branch was a quiet town.

JUST DAY TO DAY . . .

On Jan. 19, 2012, our 30th wedding anniversary, my sister Harriet, age 87, died in Calabasas, California. Ever since she had undergone open-heart surgery in 2011, I telephoned her several times a month. Harriet had been doing well and remaining in touch was a joy. Time moves on, we age and ultimately the inevitable happens. Due to the medication I had been taking my physician thought traveling to California for the funeral would be unwise. My son Kimball was able to attend. Harriet's son, Gary, the Rabbi of a congregation in Miami, Florida conducted the service.

I wrote,

Harriet you are not gone. You will always be with me, with your children, and all who have shared your life. As I think of you the first word that enters my mind is love. You and I have had the good fortune to be born into a circle of a cherished heritage, parents and grandparents whose kindness, charity, and hope showed us how to honor love and family. Though we spent many years separated by several thousands of miles our hearts could not have been closer. They will forever remain close.

We miss you!

Shelby and Christa

We also sent two photographs to be present during the service. One was a wonderful picture of my sister visiting Insel Haus on the occasion of my 80th birthday. The second photo was taken on the same day. It shows a gathering of 14 of us: my wife, children, grandchildren, and great- grandchildren, a virtual vision of the United Nations.

A happy occasion. Always close, whatever the geographic distance.

Sadly, among those missing from the group photograph is my sister Marilyn. The call from California many years ago had been earth-shattering. My 39-year-old sister Marilyn had died of a massive heart attack. My niece and nephew had lost their mother. As far as we knew there was no family history that could have made us aware of her serious health problems. We learned she'd been under tremendous stress. Mother and Dad insisted I come to California and deliver the eulogy. It was extraordinarily difficult. I could barely speak and control myself. I spoke of her love for her family, all of us, and what a loss this was.

Mother never recovered from Marilyn's death. She died in 1978 at the age of 70. Her death was due to a rare form of leukemia. Unlike Dad she'd never been able to quit smoking. There was no suffering. She was simply exhausted, entered the hospital, fell asleep, and never awakened. Dad, of course, was devastated. He too was a smoker, but he had the fortitude to quit at 40. Cold turkey!

My little sister Marilyn. Loving and playful, always the pinup!

JUST DAY TO DAY . . .

Sometime after mother's death Dad entered a home for the Jewish aged and developed a relationship with a woman who worked there. Her name was Fania. They fell in love and eloped to Las Vegas. Many years later, after both my dad and Fania had died, I received a letter from Fania's granddaughter. She'd gone through her grandmother's papers and had found photographs she thought I might like to see. She took the time and effort to find me and asked if I would like her to forward them. What a find! These are pictures I'd never seen; more pictures I cherish! Pictures of my parents and fraternal grandmother and her children. I see them every day as they hang on our wall at Insel Haus. Here's my dad, Lou, probably 20 years old. The picture clearly reveals he was one tough young man. A wise guy.

A wonderful gift. My fraternal grandmother, my dad, his brothers and sister.

Rachel and Lou Newhouse. Mother and Dad. One tough young man.

And now Phyllis' picture is lovingly displayed among family photos in our Bois Blanc Island home. When she died, we held a memorial service for her at Insel Haus. Kim was living in California. He was unable to attend. Dana had a wonderfully creative idea. He prepared a list of everything he remembered his mother loved. As we were sharing memories tough ironworker Marc stood up, said "I'm going to bed" and went upstairs. Dana, Christa, Erin, and I had a great time continuing to recall Phyllis' reaction to the many things she loved.

Phyllis in her 70s. A beloved mother, always smiling, forever young at heart.

Cleaning old records and files also reveals all kinds of events, records, even tributes. I'd forgotten this one from the Detroit Producers Association:

As a founding DPA member, Shelby has made an important contribution to the production community through the years. Because of his vision, hard work, and willingness to share his experience and expertise, the DPA proposes Shelby Newhouse as our representative to be honored at the first "Creatives for a Cure" event. We want this first "Creatives for a Cure" honor to go to one of our finest, and Shelby Newhouse is just such a person.

Today Christa and I drove to Lake Mary to enjoy an annual island party. Bring a dish to pass. There must have been 200 people there. Four guitars playing. We walked down to the beach. Christa and I sat on a pontoon boat. What a sight! Beautiful. Seeing her against a deep blue sky.

Yesterday my edition of TIME magazine arrived. The cover story? Man's trip to Mars! I couldn't help reflect on my trip from the East River of the Bronx to this moment. Who'd have thunk it? For me, just as far!

A stop along the way. San Francisco long ago. Different water, different sky, same feeling. What a sight. Beautiful.

Christa was born in Berlin, Germany. It was Hitler's Germany, Aug. 5, 1940. The political and emotional environment produced an unfortunate effect on a sensitive intelligent child. She was forever fearful, suspicious, and uncomfortable in the presence of authority figures. As a result, Christa lived, worked, and remained in America from 1964 to 2011 as a foreigner. She carried the politically correct green card for 47 years permitting this status. The presidential race of 2012 would pit President Barak Obama against a Republican candidate. She so desperately wanted to be able to vote in the coming election in support of Obama she overcame her fear of authority. Christa applied for citizenship, studied for the examination, took the required test, and passed.

On Oct. 27, we traveled 600 miles to Calumet in Michigan's Upper Peninsula for her swearing-in ceremony. This was a truly emotional experience. I, like most of us, had become a citizen the easy way having been born in the U.S. There is a difference when citizenship is bestowed as the result of a personal deliberate decision to embrace our country. President Obama now would have two votes from the Newhouse family! Today was a red-letter day for Christa. Today she cast her first vote. We are at Insel Haus on the Island. It's been a very emotional day.

ON THE ROAD AGAIN!

Monica had made arrangements to continue her physical therapy education in Austin, Texas. The three of us took off for this long-awaited trip. It was great! We could now visit our daughter Tania and her husband Trace again. And best of all, the twins would be reunited. What happened next was unbelievable. Not an auspicious beginning and a graphic example of problems in Detroit. First the Garmin, our GPS system, sent us to Canada! This meant we were driving through the Motor City where some of the street signs had lost screws, so they were hanging upside down. We read a sign that indicated a turn to the left when we knew it should have directed us to the right!

We reprogrammed the Garmin, followed I-75 South for 500 miles and spent the night in Bowling Green, Kentucky. Let me now point out a condition Christa was experiencing. She should have been visiting her ophthalmologist, not driving to Texas. Christa found it difficult to see well. Passing trucks in rainstorms became a harrowing chore. Monica vowed never again to become a passenger in her mother's car. In fact, Moe soon became her co-pilot and did a wonderful job. The next night we were in Texarkana, Texas. Soon it was Dallas. When we drove past Waco, memories of Fort Hood and Infantry Basic returned. Hard to believe what happened next. Nature was calling and I got out at a great truck stop. After using the men's stall, I found it impossible to remove the toilet paper from the device on the wall. Hey, I couldn't leave the stall without that paper. I was so angry I tore the unit off the wall! Got the paper! This had taken so long Christa had become worried about me. I exited to find her inside the truck stop waiting for me.

Arrival at Tania and Trace's Austin home was like arriving at our own home. Moe had her bedroom, we had ours, and everything was hunky-dory! Their home is spacious, welcoming, and warm. It was so satisfying to see the lifestyle they're sharing. But travel complications continued. Technology failed. Yes, we were in fact in the Lone Star State, but our expensive Garmin refused to believe it! It wouldn't accept the fact that Texas even existed. We were told it would take three days to correct the instrument. Meanwhile, Christa had to learn how to drive Moe to school. Using an ancient technique, I think it used to be called a map, Trace helped Christa plot a route to Moe's destination where she was registered to attend classes. Since Monica was learning new spine manipulation techniques she practiced them each evening on her twin, Tania.

"Nice hat"! That phrase introduces another stroke of luck. It was November 2012. Our dear friend Sheila McElligott asked if we would help her.

The problem? If she didn't use the free week timeshare coupon for the luxurious Grand Mayan Resort given to her by longtime friends, part of the "Crazy Eight" group that have been friends since her high school days, she would lose this year's visit. We had the time available, so we asked where we'd have to go? Cancún, Mexico! We didn't speak Spanish, but we did have our passports and sure would like to help Sheila. Our friend also offered travel costs including airfare, food, and incidentals. And, gee, it would be a chance to test our Homeland Security measures! They passed the test, but it did cost me my small pocketknife labeled Screen Actors Guild.

The American Airlines flight was smooth. Since our hostess traveled on an electric scooter we were always at the head of the line, receiving first class treatment. The resort . . . fantastic! Sheila, Christa, and I shared a suite that looked like a movie set. Our bedrooms were separate; there were hundreds of yards of winding pools, miles of sandy beaches, and the Gulf of Mexico! The weather was warm, not hot. The grounds were filled with tropical plants, trees, and birds. A small animal we had never seen before greeted us each morning, standing on its hind legs, begging for food. The staff was friendly and very professional.

Dinner in a very romantic setting included a unique musical treat. A solo trumpet player. He was the finest I had ever heard. Wonderful tone, pitch, and phrasing! We had a great time identifying the songs, old standards. Yes, dinner was first rate. Another dinner was accompanied by a solo violinist. We enjoyed the music, but it was an example of how today's technology puts musicians out of work. An orchestra's recording made expressly for this purpose backed up the gifted live violinist. One day I wore my pirate shirt and Sheila's large black fedora with a huge brim. As we exited our building an attractive woman called out, "Nice hat!" At 86 I could only smile.

Our weeklong visit included an all-day trip to an archaeological dig at Chichén Itzá. This was the site of an ancient Mayan village. The tour guide was excellent. His knowledge of Mayan history and religion coupled with a great sense of humor held everyone's interest. We saw a sinkhole, cenote, and had a picnic where the waiters delivered a table fully set with silverware and plates to a lower level since there was no way Sheila could climb the stairs and there was no ramp.

One evening we had the good fortune of attending a Mexican Fiesta. The food was outstanding, and the show did hold my interest. Wouldn't take much to describe the beautiful dancers' costumes! To top it off all ladies in the audience were given a colorful scarf. Each man received a straw hat. Christa liked mine. Her comment? Nice hat!

Earlier in the year, Beth Beson, our friend and benefactor, invited us to attend a high school musical. It prompted my writing and mailing the

ON THE ROAD AGAIN!

following.

April 20, 2012

Robert Watson, Principal
Northville High School
45700 6 Mile Road
Northville, Michigan 48168

Dear Mr. Watson,

Last night I had the pleasure of attending Northville High School's performance of "Hair Spray." I thank and commend you and your staff for your wisdom, courage, and inspiring selection of this ambitious project. As an 85-year-old Detroiter I am intimately aware of our racial history. I may have been the only member of Friday night's audience who applauded the splendid performance with tears in his eyes.

I was at the foot of the Belle Isle Bridge to witness the start of the 1943 riot. I returned from a trip to Canada in 1967 to see smoke rising from Detroit. It was the beginning of another race riot. Now, I've lived long enough to be part of a multi-cultural audience responding enthusiastically to a 1962 musical with a storyline making a statement about racial segregation and supporting a multi-cultural community. Last night's program gives one hope for the future.

Your orchestra's conductor and his players were great! The entire production was inspirational. Thank you, thank you, and thank you.

Shelby Newhouse

April 24, 2012

Mary Kay Pryce
Northville High School
Choir Director

Dear Mr. Newhouse,

I can't thank you enough for taking the time to write us such an incredibly thoughtful letter. We receive very little feedback about performances at the High School and your enthusiasm for our project is encouraging! It was amazing to work with the kids on this project and to try to interpret the times for them. There were so many references in the show that had to be explained since they weren't living during that era.

My Dad (born in 1924) grew up on Russell and Canfield and would talk about his life as a boy there. He would talk about playing ball in the alleys and selling newspapers near Hastings Street. His mother ran a bar on Bates St. in downtown and my dad worked there as a young man. He was also a WWII vet serving in the Philippines. Because of his commitment to family, his awesome humor, and a steady work ethic, I grew up with a great respect for the men of your generation.

I lived up on the west side of the city and graduated from Cass Tech in 1973. I was also a music major at the school, singing in the choirs and playing clarinet in the band and orchestra. I learned so much about hard work and focus, but I also remember that Velma Froude's stern approach was too much for me at that point in life, so Harp and Vocal just wasn't for me! Aren't we lucky to have had the opportunity to study at such a place?

I went on to graduate from Wayne State in 1977 and have been teaching in Northville ever since. (I remember having to ask where in the world Northville was when I applied for the job.) It's been an amazing ride to work with kids for the last 34 years.

My mom told a story about being on a bus during the riots in the 40s and I of course was around in 1967. So you can see there was so much in your letter that really hit me. Thank you for sharing your thoughts with us all. It would be an honor to meet you personally if there's ever a chance. Our Spring Concert is on Wed. and Thurs. May 16 and May 17 at 7:00 p.m. If you're able to come please let me know and I'll reserve some tickets for you.

Respectfully yours,

Mary Kay Pryce
NHS Choir director

ON THE ROAD AGAIN!

April 30, 2012

Dear Mary Kay,

Thank you for your response to my review of your "Hair Spray" production. It was a most important evening for you, your cast, and me. Another Cass Tech music major! Would you believe I remember Velma Froude and her harp classes? I was playing French horn. What a faculty we had! Our French horn teacher, Francis Hellstein was first chair for the Detroit Symphony. Only those of us who attended Cass can fully appreciate the full meaning of that experience. I returned from World War II with a wife and child. Went right to work. Never went to college. Cass was the extent of my formal education. I'm enclosing a resume of films I have made. Whatever measure of success I've achieved I know I must attribute much of it to Cass.

Your Dad may have heard me before returning from the Philippines. In 1945 I was a member of WVTR, Armed Forces Radio broadcasting from the same studio used by the infamous Tokyo Rose. His recollections of growing up in Detroit mirror mine. Playing ball in the alleys and delivering newspapers. I can add to that playing in the streets of the Bronx and swimming in New York's East River.

Wish I could be here to enjoy your Spring Concert, but tomorrow we depart Farmington Hills at 7 a.m. for the 4-hour drive to Cheboygan to catch the ferry to Bois Blanc Island. The next six months will be spent running Insel Haus our B&B on the island. Please view our web site: inselhausbandb.com. Mary Kay, keep up the good work.

Shelby

Last night Christa and I were in the audience of the Farmington Players community theater. The show, "The 1940's Radio Hour" was a musical comedy. As I had worked the night shift at WJLB in 1943 I was intrigued and we bought tickets. It was a thoroughly enjoyable evening. But what was particularly memorable was what happened as we left the theater. When I congratulated one of the actresses she extended her hand. I quickly said I no longer shook the hands of ladies. I gave her a hug and explained I was 86 years old. The fellow standing next to me said he was also 86. We chatted outside the theater, and I learned he had been a staff announcer at WJR when I worked at WWJ. We knew many of Detroit's radio-television performers between 1950 and 1980. Though I didn't remember his name he did remember me. There may have been 300 in that evening's audience. We drove home while I wondered how out of the huge number leaving the theater he and I had found each other. I have experienced many synchronistic events. This was another example. I keep thinking of that book in my library titled, "There Is No Such Thing as a Coincidence."

It's the first of May and we are back on the island. The past winter was spent at our home in Farmington Hills, Michigan. This has been the only winter during the past 10 years we've not been at Insel Haus. The combination of my advanced age, coupled with the absence of medical facilities on Bois Blanc and the difficulties associated with getting off the island during the winter to attend to any medical emergency dictated our stay in Farmington Hills.

The other day Christa drove to our southern home. She and our Chinese friend, Li Hong had been preparing Insel Haus for the coming 2012 season. This led to an interesting encounter. They drove off. Now I'd be alone operating Insel Haus for two days and one night. Two guests would arrive. LeRoy would spend the night and then do work for the township. I also had a list of chores for Carl, the plumber. I overlooked the note indicating Carl would arrive in two days, on Thursday. Sheila, our friend and guest was also at Insel Haus. This provided me with a dog fix since her miniature Dachshund, Freda #5, accompanied her. The scene was set for a comedy of errors.

The next morning a man arrived wearing a T-shirt. I was profiling. He didn't look like a man ready to do office work for the township. I welcomed him thinking he was Carl the plumber, thanked him for coming, and said follow me. I'll show you some of the things that need to be done. This friendly fellow followed me upstairs to a bathroom where I pointed out a toilet that was leaking. He still hadn't said a word. Next we looked at our wonderful Jacuzzi bathroom.

"Carl," I said, "this has got to be fixed. The Jacuzzi has a leak."

"Wait a minute," the plumber said. "I don't think so."

"But Christa put it on the list," I said.

"Mr. Newhouse, you keep calling me Carl. My name is LeRoy."

I began to laugh. I'd expected LeRoy to be a man in a suit! We went back downstairs and started all over again. Sheila was also laughing. I'm convinced Frieda #5 was enjoying this charade. LeRoy had a great stay, loved his room, and looked forward to returning with his wife.

Breakfast provided another opportunity for me to demonstrate I was not quite ready to take over. We now owned a new coffee maker. I couldn't find a way to turn it on. I used my cell phone to call Christa to describe the message that appeared on the machine. "Do Not Operate Unless Adult Supervisor Is Present." I asked Christa where I could find an adult. We both laughed at that one! I learned the start button was at the rear of the unit. LeRoy enjoyed three great cups of coffee.

This past week Alan, our painter from Livonia, has been putting a different color and new coat of paint on all of our decks: front, rear, 2nd floor and exterior staircase. He has had two recent island experiences I must recount. Alan will surely carry his story back to civilization. It was after 9 in the evening. Having worked all day in 90-degree heat he was cooling off at the beach in front of Insel Haus. Though after 9 p.m. it was still fairly light. The strange sound he heard was a deer, a buck snorting, stomping his feet, waving his antlers. The deer's target? Alan! Clearly our innocent painter had invaded his territory. There was not a doe in sight. This was not about a sexual conquest. Just as you and I know every piece of furniture in our living room that buck knew his territory like the palm of his hoof. Who or what was this stranger in his living room? Though Alan was moved by this display he did stand his ground. Proof life can be stranger than fiction, no sooner had the disturbed animal moved off, Al experienced something neither we nor anyone else we knew of had ever experienced. A huge adult duck flew into the tall Norway pine next to him. Fell dead at his feet! We would have doubted Al's story, but the beautiful huge fowl was indeed on our beach. The evidence was there. We left it for others in this environment to properly dispose of it in the usual way.

Another Alpaca show. Hand spun, hand knitted sweater. One of my favorites.

Christa attended an art show on the island recently and exhibited beautifully knitted garments and beaded jewelry. A precocious 9-year-old girl made the following observation. I believe it was absolutely precious and worthy of sharing. Christa had had a great experience with this little girl when they met two years ago at our Insel Haus Wednesday night get-togethers. Christa had shown her how to spin, ply, and wash the yarn, and had given her the resulting skein as a gift.

So, at this year's art show she came by and said: "Hello Miss Christa, I just wanted to say 'Hi'." It took us a little while to recognize Taylor. She had grown a bit and sounded very adult. During this short visit she told another little girl what Christa does and how much goes into making the pieces she had for sale.

> First Christa has to raise the Alpacas, then she has to shear them, then she has to spin the yarn, then she has to dye the yarn, then she has to design the piece, then she has to knit the piece and then the people walk by and look at the price and say RIP OFF!!!

What a great commercial for HAND MADE IN AMERICA. And all told by a 9-year-old with a slight lisp. It made Christa's day.

Aug. 9, 2013. Surprise! Some surprises are greater than others. This one took the cake! Christa and I drove to the dock to pick up Moe, scheduled to arrive on today's 8 a.m. boat. Christa sat in our car, and I walked to the docking Kristen D to greet her. Wow! I thought I was looking at a photograph! Moe was approaching with her twin sister, Tania, the hospice nurse from Austin, Texas!!! What an unexpected and marvelous surprise! Imagine her mother's reaction as we approached the car. This was Tania's first visit to Insel Haus and Bois Blanc Island since my 80th birthday six years ago! Her husband Trace was attending a convention in Chicago. Moe knew of the plan. Her sister was to drive to Cheboygan, spend the night with her and surprise us this morning. They kept the plan secret. We couldn't have been more shocked! This didn't make our day. It made our year!!! While sitting here writing this, both girls are doing my work. Vacuuming! Yes, like your mom, am I glad to see you!!!

ALMOST FULL CIRCLE
(My past has made my present possible)

A few days ago, Christa and I visited the Holocaust Center in Bloomfield Hills. We were met by several docents, a few other adults, and about a hundred kids! Must have been several classes from local schools. We were broken into several smaller groups and off we went. Our leader, a man of about 70, asked us, "Is there anyone here from another country?" Christa spoke up. "Yes." "Where are you from"? Since she was born in Berlin she answered, "Germany." He may have been surprised, but that didn't stop him. He then spent several minutes attempting to recreate the desperate times in Germany after the ending of the First World War and signing of the Versailles Treaty.

He then asked if any of us remembered Father Coughlin. "Yes!" I called out. "His beautiful National Shrine of the Little Flower still stands on Woodward Avenue in Detroit." The docent then pointed to an exhibit of printed flyers written by that priest in the 1920s and '30s. These were diatribes of antisemitic literature. Father Coughlin, the Radio Priest as he became known, signed a contract with CBS. Estimates gave him almost 40 million listeners. I was old enough to understand some of the import of what was happening. A wave of antisemitism was underway, sweeping the country. Fortunately, when Father Coughlin began praising Adolph Hitler in 1940, he was already losing followers. His vile actions were brought to the attention of church leaders. Rome responded to his growing notoriety and the Vatican withdrew his ability to continue as a priest. At that time, I was 13 and aware of his activities.

I spoke to the Holocaust Museum group of my experience as a boy growing up in Detroit. Remember seeing a sign outside of an apartment building advertising apartments for rent. It read, "No dogs or Jews allowed!" I turned to an African American lady and said she would have lived in Paradise Valley where her rent would have been twice or three times that paid by a Caucasian family living in the same kind of housing. "Yes," she said. Her sister had told her of that. I wondered, have times changed since then?

Our group moved through a series of various exhibits. They detailed how millions of men, women, and children were killed, subjected to medical experiments, forced to work till they died, or were freed as virtual skeletons by victorious Allied troops in 1944. We studied an actual railroad car that had transported Jews from their home country as the German armies overran Europe.

I was reminded of an experience I had more than 40 years ago. I was invited to address a group of women about my "Heritage" film. In the middle of my talk, an elderly woman with a heavy European accent shouted out, "Why not a film about Jews, about Hitler? Not black people!" Others hushed her and I'm ashamed to say I was startled and too young to compose a good response. I should have left the dais, gone to her and embraced her. Greeted her with the Hebrew expression, shalom aleichem, peace be upon you. Told her in Yiddish I knew of her pain. She could easily have been an immigrant who had escaped Hitler's wrath. I regret I didn't tell her I shared her pain.

There's a marvelous story of a man who once stood before God, his heart breaking from the pain and injustice in the world. "Dear God," he cried out, "look at all the suffering, the anguish and distress in the world. Why don't you send help?" God said, "I did send help. I sent you."

I do believe in following the principal inherent in that tale. To be an activist engaged in the fight to right injustice and not to simply stand by and accept injustice.

Where did I get my life-long penchant for protection of the rights, the loves, the lives of others? I believe my past made my present possible. Think for a moment of Lou, my dad. Brought to the U.S. at the age of 4. I bet he never became a citizen. Don't remember ever hearing of such a thing. Running away from home at 14. Me? I waited 'til I was 17.

My vocabulary is inadequate when it comes to describing how incredibly fortunate I've been throughout my life. I have had problems, of course, but as I review the overcoming of setbacks, our ability always to go on, my marriage to Phyllis, partnership with Christa, our six children, grandchildren, great-grandchildren, good health, and the fact that I'm able to share this history, what more could one ask for? I'm convinced I was being conditioned for my lifelong sympathy for the plight of the underdog. Look at the societal issues I've supported. I recognize my extraordinarily good fortune in finding opportunities to work on projects contributing to the advancement of ideas, informing and improving the lives of others. And by the way, I do continue to wonder what it'll feel like when I get old . . .

Shalom Aleichem, dear reader.

Affectionately,

Shelby Ziel Newhouse

ALMOST FULL CIRCLE

1926 - 2020

SHELBY ALWAYS KNEW HOW TO SAY
"Thank You"

Getting his story on "paper" and published was one of Shelby's dreams. And like every project he undertook, he knew it would take more than his effort, authorship, talent and labor to make it possible. Now his dream has been realized and thank-yous are in order.

Gratitude to those involved in bringing his book to fruition would probably be expressed more elegantly by the author himself, but a simple, heartfelt thank you will need to suffice.

THANK YOU ALL!

With a special thank you to . . .

Christa Kindt Newhouse, for your life-long love and support and yeoman job as producer, researcher, archivist, manuscript editor, and project manager.

Paula McKinney Tucker, for your forever friendship, co-producing, intuitive editing, organizing and layout of my story.

Dana Ingersoll Newhouse, for your encouragement, counsel, legal research and advice during every iteration.

Steve Kruk for your beautiful cover treatment, logo design, proofing, and expertise used to shepherd the book through publishing.

SOURCE NOTES

HOW IT ALL STARTED (p. 1-4)

p. 1 Fromm, B. (1990). Blood & Banquets: A Berlin Social Diary. Birch Lane Press.

p. 2 Altenhof, A. CCBY-SA 4.0 via Wikimedia Commons. URL:
https: commons.wikimedia.org/wiki/File:Europe-1878-map-en.png

FIVE MONTHS LATER. . . (p. 23-28)

p. 25 Ambrose, S. E. (2002, Nov. 19). To America: Personal Reflections of an Historian. Simon and Schuster.

BACK ON THE AIR (p. 29-34)

p. 32 Newhouse, S. N. (2001) WVTR Memories, The Co-operative Global Radio Memories Project, Radio Heritage Foundation.
http://www.radioheritage.net/Story33.asp

Newhouse, S. N. (2001, April 30) AFRA Armed Forces Radio Memories, "Radio Tokyo-WVTR." Memorable Radio, The Co-operative Global Radio Memories Project, Radio Heritage Foundation. https://www.radioheritage.com/radio-tokyo-wvtr/

PUTTING DOWN ROOTS Thank you Detroit News (p. 39-42)

p. 41 The Detroit News. (1952)

WHAT ELSE BUT AUTOMOTIVE? (p. 51-62)

p. 51 Railton, A. (1950s) Popular Mechanics.

MEADOW BROOK HALL (p. 63-68)

p. 63 (1931, Monday, May 25) "Business and Finance: Women in Banking." Time.

INEQUALITY AND EQUAL JUSTICE (p. 69-78)

p. 69 King Jr., M. L. (1955) Montgomery Bus Boycott.

p. 72 Hoberman, J. (2004) Interview, The Boston Globe.

IT'S ONLY POLITICS (p. 95-100)

p. 95 Pavich, R. M. (1974, Oct. 31, Thursday) A film flop. The Detroit News. Page 3, Section A.

p. 97 Levy, D. S. (1997) Two-Gun Cohen A Biography. Thomas Dunne Books/ St. Martin's Press.

McClintock, P. (2011, April 13) Bieber Entertainment Enterprises Purchases Rights to 'Chinese General.' The Hollywood Reporter.

https://www.hollywoodreporter.com/movies/movie-news/bieber-entertainment-enterprises-purchases-screen-177990/

A LIGHTNING ROD FOR CONTROVERSY *(p. 101-108)*

p. 104 Rivera, D. (1932) The Detroit News.

CHANGES ALL AROUND *(p. 117-126)*

p. 122 Marchel, C. (1987, Spring) Detroit's Unique Support System. Media Community Rallies Behind Christa Kindt. Zooming In, Vol. 19, Issue 2.

p. 126 Gibbons, D. (1997) Christa's Excellent Adventure. Michigan VUE.

SECRETS AND THE CURSE *(p. 135-142)*

p. 135 Crowdy, M. (Rev.), Fraser, H. (1981, Oct.) translation: Interview with Pope John Paul II. Approaches.

The Fatima Center. Pope John Paul II in Fulda, Germany (1980). Published Testimony. Stimme des Glaubens.

Putti, F. (Fr) (1981, Oct.) Interview with Pope John Paul II. Chiesa Viva.

p. 140 De Jonge, A. (1982) The Life and Times of Gregorii Rasputin. Coward, McCann and Geoghegan.

OMNE TRIUM PERFECTUM. . . *Good Things Come in Threes* *(p .143-148)*

p. 143-44 Dominguez, L., Ray, C., Starko, K., Stromberg, W., Woodall, D. (1980, Dec. 1) Reye's Syndrome and Salicylate Use. Pediatrics, 66 (6).

FRIENDS! *(p. 163-168)*

p. 166 King, A. (2002, Oct. 22). Alan King's Great Jewish Joke Book. Crown.

Twain, M. (1884, Dec.10) Adventures of Huckleberry Finn. Chatto and Windus/ Charles L. Webster and Company.